Unity 5.x Game AI Programming Cookbook

Build and customize a wide range of powerful Unity AI systems with over 70 hands-on recipes and techniques

Jorge Palacios

[PACKT]
PUBLISHING

BIRMINGHAM - MUMBAI

Unity 5.x Game AI Programming Cookbook

First published: March 2016

Production reference: 1230316

Published by Packt Publishing Ltd.
Livery Place
35 Livery Street
Birmingham B3 2PB, UK.

ISBN 978-1-78355-357-0

www.packtpub.com

Cover image by Andrés Rodolfo De León Mariola (andresvdlm@hotmail.com)

Credits

Author
Jorge Palacios

Reviewers
Jack Donovan
Lauren S. Ferro

Commissioning Editor
Akram Hussain

Acquisition Editors
Mohammad Rizvi
Usha Iyer

Content Development Editor
Kirti Patil

Technical Editor
Deepti Tuscano

Copy Editor
Angad Singh

Project Coordinator
Nidhi Joshi

Proofreader
Safis Editing

Indexer
Monica Ajmera Mehta

Production Coordinator
Arvindkumar Gupta

Cover Work
Arvindkumar Gupta

About the Author

Jorge Palacios is a software developer with seven years of professional experience. He has committed the last four years to game development working in various positions; from tool developer, to lead programmer. His main focus is AI and gameplay programming, and currently he works with Unity and HTML5. He's also a game development instructor, speaker, and game jam organizer.

You can find more about him on `http://jorge.palacios.co`

About the Reviewers

Jack Donovan is a game developer and software engineer who has been working with the Unity3D engine since its third major release. He studied at Champlain College in Burlington, Vermont, where he received a BS in game programming.

Jack currently works at IrisVR, a virtual reality startup in New York City, where he is developing software that allows architects to generate virtual reality experiences from their CAD models. Before IrisVR, Jack worked on a small independent game team with fellow students, where he wrote the book, *OUYA Game Development By Example*.

Lauren S. Ferro is a gamification consultant and designer of games and game-like applications. She has worked, designed, consulted, and implemented strategies for a range of different purposes from the fields of professional development, recommendation systems, and educational games. She is an active researcher in the area of gamification, player profiling, and user-centered game design. She runs workshops for both the general public and companies that focus on designing user-centered games and game-like applications. She is also the developer of the game design resource Gamicards, which is a paper-prototyping tool for both games and game-like experiences.

www.PacktPub.com

eBooks, discount offers, and more

Did you know that Packt offers eBook versions of every book published, with PDF and ePub files available? You can upgrade to the eBook version at www.PacktPub.com and as a print book customer, you are entitled to a discount on the eBook copy. Get in touch with us at customercare@packtpub.com for more details.

At www.PacktPub.com, you can also read a collection of free technical articles, sign up for a range of free newsletters and receive exclusive discounts and offers on Packt books and eBooks.

https://www2.packtpub.com/books/subscription/packtlib

Do you need instant solutions to your IT questions? PacktLib is Packt's online digital book library. Here, you can search, access, and read Packt's entire library of books.

Why subscribe?

- ‣ Fully searchable across every book published by Packt
- ‣ Copy and paste, print, and bookmark content
- ‣ On demand and accessible via a web browser

Table of Contents

Preface

When we think about artificial intelligence, a lot of topics may come to mind. From simple behaviors such as following or escaping from the player, through the classical Chess-rival AI, to state-of-the-art techniques in Machine Learning or procedural content generation.

Talking about Unity means talking about game development democratization. Thanks to its ease of use, fast-paced technological improvement, an ever-growing community of developers, and the new cloud services offered, Unity has become one of the most important game industry software.

With all that in mind, the main goal in writing this book is to offer you, the reader, both technical insight into Unity, following best practices and conventions, and theoretical knowledge that help you grasp artificial intelligence concepts and techniques, so you could get the best of both worlds for your own personal and professional development.

This cookbook will introduce you to the tools to build great AI; either for creating better enemies, polishing that final boss, or even building your own customized AI engine. It aims to be your one-stop reference for developing artificial intelligence techniques in Unity.

Welcome to an exciting journey that combines a variety of things that means a lot to me as a professional and human being; programming, game development, artificial intelligence, and sharing knowledge with other developers. I cannot stress how humbled and happy I am to be read by you right now, and grateful to the team at Packt for this formidable opportunity. I hope this material helps you not only take your Unity and artificial intelligence skills to new levels, but also deliver that feature that will engage players into your game.

What this book covers

Chapter 1, Behaviors – Intelligent Movement, explores some of the most interesting movement algorithms based on the steering behavior principles developed by Craig Reynolds along with work from Ian Millington. They act as a foundation for most of the AI used in advanced games and other algorithms that rely on movement, such as the family of path-finding algorithms.

Chapter 2, Navigation, explores path-finding algorithms for navigating complex scenarios. It will include some ways to represent the world using different kinds of graph structures, and several algorithms for finding a path, each aimed at different situations.

Chapter 3, Decision Making, shows the different decision-making techniques that are flexible enough to adapt to different types of games, and robust enough to let us build modular decision-making systems.

Chapter 4, Coordination and Tactics, deals with a number of different recipes for coordinating different agents as a whole organism, such as formations and techniques that allow us make tactical decisions based on graphs, such as waypoints and influence maps.

Chapter 5, Agent Awareness, deals with different approaches of simulating sense stimuli on an agent. We will learn how to use tools that we already know to create these simulations, colliders, and graphs.

Chapter 6, Board Games AI, explains a family of algorithms for developing board-game techniques to create artificial intelligence.

Chapter 7, Learning Techniques, explores the field of machine learning. It will give us a great head start in our endeavor to learn and apply machine-learning techniques to our games.

Chapter 8, Miscellaneous, introduces new techniques and uses algorithms that we have learned about in previous chapters in order to create new behaviors that don't quite fit in a definite category.

What you need for this book

The examples were tested and are provided using the latest version of Unity by the time of finishing this material, which is Unity 5.3.4f1. However, the book content started its development on Unity 5.1.2, so this is the minimum recommended version to work with.

Who this book is for

This book is aimed at those who already have basic knowledge of Unity and are eager to get more tools under their belt in order to solve AI and gameplay-related problems.

Sections

In this book, you will find several headings that appear frequently (Getting ready, How to do it, How it works, There's more, and See also).

To give clear instructions on how to complete a recipe, we use these sections as follows:

Getting ready

This section tells you what to expect in the recipe, and describes how to set up any software or any preliminary settings required for the recipe.

How to do it...

This section contains the steps required to follow the recipe.

How it works...

This section usually consists of a detailed explanation of what happened in the previous section.

There's more...

This section consists of additional information about the recipe in order to make the reader more knowledgeable about the recipe.

See also

This section provides helpful links to other useful information for the recipe.

Conventions

In this book, you will find a number of text styles that distinguish between different kinds of information. Here are some examples of these styles and an explanation of their meaning.

Code words in text, database table names, folder names, filenames, file extensions, pathnames, dummy URLs, user input, and Twitter handles are shown as follows: "AgentBehaviour is the template class for most of the behaviors covered in the chapter."

A block of code is set as follows:

```
using UnityEngine;
using System.Collections;
public class Steering
{
    public float angular;
    public Vector3 linear;
    public Steering ()
    {
        angular = 0.0f;
        linear = new Vector3();
    }
}
```

When we wish to draw your attention to a particular part of a code block, the relevant lines or items are set in bold:

```
using UnityEngine;
using System.Collections;

public class Wander : Face
{
    public float offset;
    public float radius;
    public float rate;
}
```

Warnings or important notes appear in a box like this.

Tips and tricks appear like this.

Reader feedback

Feedback from our readers is always welcome. Let us know what you think about this book—what you liked or disliked. Reader feedback is important for us as it helps us develop titles that you will really get the most out of.

To send us general feedback, simply e-mail feedback@packtpub.com, and mention the book's title in the subject of your message.

If there is a topic that you have expertise in and you are interested in either writing or contributing to a book, see our author guide at www.packtpub.com/authors.

Customer support

Now that you are the proud owner of a Packt book, we have a number of things to help you to get the most from your purchase.

Downloading the example code

You can download the example code files for this book from your account at
`http://www.packtpub.com`. If you purchased this book elsewhere, you can visit
`http://www.packtpub.com/support` and register to have the files e-mailed
directly to you.

You can download the code files by following these steps:

1. Log in or register to our website using your e-mail address and password.
2. Hover the mouse pointer on the **SUPPORT** tab at the top.
3. Click on **Code Downloads & Errata**.
4. Enter the name of the book in the **Search** box.
5. Select the book for which you're looking to download the code files.
6. Choose from the drop-down menu where you purchased this book from.
7. Click on **Code Download**.

Once the file is downloaded, please make sure that you unzip or extract the folder using the
latest version of:

- WinRAR / 7-Zip for Windows
- Zipeg / iZip / UnRarX for Mac
- 7-Zip / PeaZip for Linux

Downloading the color images of this book

We also provide you with a PDF file that has color images of the screenshots/diagrams used
in this book. The color images will help you better understand the changes in the output.
You can download this file from `http://www.packtpub.com/sites/default/files/`
`downloads/Unity5xGameAIProgrammingCookbook_ColorImages.pdf`.

Errata

Although we have taken every care to ensure the accuracy of our content, mistakes do happen.
If you find a mistake in one of our books—maybe a mistake in the text or the code—we would be
grateful if you could report this to us. By doing so, you can save other readers from frustration
and help us improve subsequent versions of this book. If you find any errata, please report them
by visiting `http://www.packtpub.com/submit-errata`, selecting your book, clicking on
the **Errata Submission Form** link, and entering the details of your errata. Once your errata are
verified, your submission will be accepted and the errata will be uploaded to our website or
added to any list of existing errata under the Errata section of that title.

To view the previously submitted errata, go to https://www.packtpub.com/books/content/support and enter the name of the book in the search field. The required information will appear under the **Errata** section.

Piracy

Piracy of copyrighted material on the Internet is an ongoing problem across all media. At Packt, we take the protection of our copyright and licenses very seriously. If you come across any illegal copies of our works in any form on the Internet, please provide us with the location address or website name immediately so that we can pursue a remedy.

Please contact us at copyright@packtpub.com with a link to the suspected pirated material.

We appreciate your help in protecting our authors and our ability to bring you valuable content.

Questions

If you have a problem with any aspect of this book, you can contact us at questions@packtpub.com, and we will do our best to address the problem.

1
Behaviors – Intelligent Movement

In this chapter, we will develop AI algorithms for movement by covering the following recipes:

- ▶ Creating the behaviors' template
- ▶ Pursuing and evading
- ▶ Arriving and leaving
- ▶ Facing objects
- ▶ Wandering around
- ▶ Following a path
- ▶ Avoiding agents
- ▶ Avoiding walls
- ▶ Blending behaviors by weight
- ▶ Blending behaviors by priority
- ▶ Combining behaviors using a steering pipeline
- ▶ Shooting a projectile
- ▶ Predicting a projectile's landing spot
- ▶ Targeting a projectile
- ▶ Creating a jump system

Introduction

Unity has been one of the most popular game engines for quite a while now, and it's probably the de facto game development tool for indie developers, not only because of its business model, which has a low entry barrier, but also because of its robust project editor, year-by-year technological improvement, and most importantly, ease of use and an ever-growing community of developers around the globe.

Thanks to Unity's heavy lifting behind the scenes (rendering, physics, integration, and cross-platform deployment, just to name a few) it's possible for us to focus on creating the AI systems that will bring to life our games, creating great real-time experiences in the blink of an eye.

The goal of this book is to give you the tools to build great AI, for creating better enemies, polishing that final boss, or even building your own customized AI engine.

In this chapter, we will start by exploring some of the most interesting movement algorithms based on the steering behavior principles developed by Craig Reynolds, along with work from Ian Millington. These recipes are the stepping stones for most of the AI used in advanced games and other algorithms that rely on movement, such as the family of path-finding algorithms.

Creating the behavior template

Before creating our behaviors, we need to code the stepping stones that help us not only to create only intelligent movement, but also to build a modular system to change and add these behaviors. We will create custom data types and base classes for most of the algorithms covered in this chapter.

Getting ready

Our first step is to remember the update function order of execution:

- ► `Update`
- ► `LateUpdate`

Also, it's important to refresh so that we can select the scripts' order of execution. For our behaviors to work as intended, the rules for ordering are as follows:

- ► Agent scripts
- ► Behavior scripts
- ► Behaviors or scripts based on the previous ones

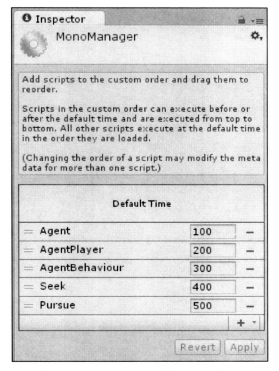

This is an example of how to arrange the order of execution for the movement scripts.
We need to pursue derives from Seek, which derives from AgentBehaviour.

How to do it...

We need to create three classes: `Steering`, `AgentBehaviour`, and `Agent`:

1. `Steering` serves as a custom data type for storing the movement and rotation of the agent:

```
using UnityEngine;
using System.Collections;
public class Steering
{
    public float angular;
    public Vector3 linear;
    public Steering ()
    {
        angular = 0.0f;
        linear = new Vector3();
    }
}
```

2. Create the `AgentBehaviour` class, which is the template class for most of the behaviors covered in this chapter:

```
using UnityEngine;
using System.Collections;
public class AgentBehaviour : MonoBehaviour
{
    public GameObject target;
    protected Agent agent;
    public virtual void Awake ()
    {
        agent = gameObject.GetComponent<Agent>();
    }
    public virtual void Update ()
    {
            agent.SetSteering(GetSteering());
    }
    public virtual Steering GetSteering ()
    {
        return new Steering();
    }
}
```

3. Finally, `Agent` is the main component, and it makes use of behaviors in order to create intelligent movement. Create the file and its barebones:

```
using UnityEngine;
using System.Collections;
public class Agent : MonoBehaviour
{
    public float maxSpeed;
    public float maxAccel;
    public float orientation;
    public float rotation;
    public Vector3 velocity;
    protected Steering steering;
    void Start ()
    {
        velocity = Vector3.zero;
        steering = new Steering();
    }
    public void SetSteering (Steering steering)
    {
        this.steering = steering;
    }
}
```

4. Next, we code the `Update` function, which handles the movement according to the current value:

```
public virtual void Update ()
{
    Vector3 displacement = velocity * Time.deltaTime;
    orientation += rotation * Time.deltaTime;
    // we need to limit the orientation values
    // to be in the range (0 - 360)
    if (orientation < 0.0f)
        orientation += 360.0f;
    else if (orientation > 360.0f)
        orientation -= 360.0f;
    transform.Translate(displacement, Space.World);
    transform.rotation = new Quaternion();
    transform.Rotate(Vector3.up, orientation);
}
```

5. Finally, we implement the `LateUpdate` function, which takes care of updating the steering for the next frame according to the current frame's calculations:

```
public virtual void LateUpdate ()
{
    velocity += steering.linear * Time.deltaTime;
    rotation += steering.angular * Time.deltaTime;
    if (velocity.magnitude > maxSpeed)
    {
        velocity.Normalize();
        velocity = velocity * maxSpeed;
    }
    if (steering.angular == 0.0f)
    {
        rotation = 0.0f;
    }
    if (steering.linear.sqrMagnitude == 0.0f)
    {
        velocity = Vector3.zero;
    }
    steering = new Steering();
}
```

How it works...

The idea is to be able to delegate the movement's logic inside the `GetSteering()` function on the behaviors that we will later build, simplifying our agent's class to a main calculation based on those.

Besides, we are guaranteed to set the agent's steering value before it is used thanks to Unity script and function execution orders.

There's more...

This is a component-based approach, which means that we have to remember to always have an `Agent` script attached to `GameObject` for the behaviors to work as expected.

See also

For further information on Unity's game loop and the execution order of functions and scripts, please refer to the official documentation available online at:

- http://docs.unity3d.com/Manual/ExecutionOrder.html
- http://docs.unity3d.com/Manual/class-ScriptExecution.html

Pursuing and evading

Pursuing and evading are great behaviors to start with because they rely on the most basic behaviors and extend their functionality by predicting the target's next step.

Getting ready

We need a couple of basic behaviors called `Seek` and `Flee`; place them right after the `Agent` class in the scripts' execution order.

The following is the code for the `Seek` behaviour:

```
using UnityEngine;
using System.Collections;
public class Seek : AgentBehaviour
{
    public override Steering GetSteering()
    {
        Steering steering = new Steering();
        steering.linear = target.transform.position - transform.
position;
```

```
            steering.linear.Normalize();
            steering.linear = steering.linear * agent.maxAccel;
            return steering;
        }
    }
```

Also, we need to implement the `Flee` behavior:

```csharp
using UnityEngine;
using System.Collections;
public class Flee : AgentBehaviour
{
    public override Steering GetSteering()
    {
        Steering steering = new Steering();
        steering.linear = transform.position - target.transform.
position;
        steering.linear.Normalize();
        steering.linear = steering.linear * agent.maxAccel;
        return steering;
    }
}
```

How to do it...

`Pursue` and `Evade` are essentially the same algorithm but differ in terms of the base class they derive from:

1. Create the `Pursue` class, derived from `Seek`, and add the attributes for the prediction:

    ```csharp
    using UnityEngine;
    using System.Collections;

    public class Pursue : Seek
    {
        public float maxPrediction;
        private GameObject targetAux;
        private Agent targetAgent;
    }
    ```

2. Implement the `Awake` function in order to set up everything according to the real target:

```
public override void Awake()
{
    base.Awake();
    targetAgent = target.GetComponent<Agent>();
    targetAux = target;
    target = new GameObject();
}
```

3. As well as implement the `OnDestroy` function, to properly handle the internal object:

```
void OnDestroy ()
{
    Destroy(targetAux);
}
```

4. Finally, implement the `GetSteering` function:

```
public override Steering GetSteering()
{
    Vector3 direction = targetAux.transform.position - transform.
position;
    float distance = direction.magnitude;
    float speed = agent.velocity.magnitude;
    float prediction;
    if (speed <= distance / maxPrediction)
        prediction = maxPrediction;
    else
        prediction = distance / speed;
    target.transform.position = targetAux.transform.position;
    target.transform.position += targetAgent.velocity *
prediction;
    return base.GetSteering();
}
```

5. To create the `Evade` behavior, the procedure is just the same, but it takes into account that `Flee` is the parent class:

```
public class Evade : Flee
{

    // everything stays the same

}
```

How it works...

These behaviors rely on `Seek` and `Flee` and take into consideration the target's velocity in order to predict where it will go next; they aim at that position using an internal extra object.

Arriving and leaving

Similar to `Seek` and `Flee`, the idea behind these algorithms is to apply the same principles and extend the functionality to a point where the agent stops automatically after a condition is met, either being close to its destination (arrive), or far enough from a dangerous point (leave).

Getting ready

We need to create one file for each of the algorithms, `Arrive` and `Leave`, respectively, and remember to set their custom execution order.

How to do it...

They use the same approach, but in terms of implementation, the name of the member variables change as well as some computations in the first half of the `GetSteering` function:

1. First, implement the `Arrive` behaviour with its member variables to define the radius for stopping (target) and slowing down:

```
using UnityEngine;
using System.Collections;

public class Arrive : AgentBehaviour
{
    public float targetRadius;
    public float slowRadius;
    public float timeToTarget = 0.1f;
}
```

2. Create the `GetSteering` function:

```
public override Steering GetSteering()
{
    // code in next steps
}
```

3. Define the first half of the `GetSteering` function, in which we compute the desired speed depending on the distance from the target according to the radii variables:

```
Steering steering = new Steering();
Vector3 direction = target.transform.position - transform.
position;
float distance = direction.magnitude;
float targetSpeed;
if (distance < targetRadius)
    return steering;
if (distance > slowRadius)
    targetSpeed = agent.maxSpeed;
else
    targetSpeed = agent.maxSpeed * distance / slowRadius;
```

4. Define the second half of the `GetSteering` function, in which we set the steering value and clamp it according to the maximum speed:

```
Vector3 desiredVelocity = direction;
desiredVelocity.Normalize();
desiredVelocity *= targetSpeed;
steering.linear = desiredVelocity - agent.velocity;
steering.linear /= timeToTarget;
if (steering.linear.magnitude > agent.maxAccel)
{
    steering.linear.Normalize();
    steering.linear *= agent.maxAccel;
}
return steering;
```

5. To implement `Leave`, the name of the member variables changes:

```
using UnityEngine;
using System.Collections;

public class Leave : AgentBehaviour
{
    public float escapeRadius;
    public float dangerRadius;
    public float timeToTarget = 0.1f;
}
```

6. Define the first half of the `GetSteering` function:

```
Steering steering = new Steering();
Vector3 direction = transform.position - target.transform.
position;
float distance = direction.magnitude;
```

```
if (distance > dangerRadius)
    return steering;
float reduce;
if (distance < escapeRadius)
    reduce = 0f;
else
    reduce = distance / dangerRadius * agent.maxSpeed;
float targetSpeed = agent.maxSpeed - reduce;
```

7. And finally, the second half of `GetSteering` stays just the same.

How it works...

After calculating the direction to go in, the next calculations are based on two radii distances in order to know when to go full throttle, slow down, and stop; that's why we have several `if` statements. In the `Arrive` behavior, when the agent is too far, we aim to full-throttle, progressively slow down when inside the proper radius, and finally to stop when close enough to the target. The converse train of thought applies to `Leave`.

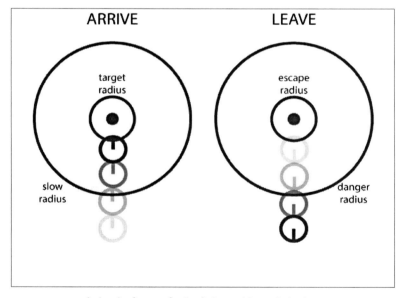

A visual reference for the Arrive and Leave behaviors

Facing objects

Real-world aiming, just like in combat simulators, works a little differently from the widely-used *automatic* aiming in almost every game. Imagine that you need to implement an agent controlling a tank turret or a humanized sniper; that's when this recipe comes in handy.

Getting ready

We need to make some modifications to our `AgentBehaviour` class:

1. Add new member values to limit some of the existing ones:

```
public float maxSpeed;
public float maxAccel;
public float maxRotation;
public float maxAngularAccel;
```

2. Add a function called `MapToRange`. This function helps in finding the actual direction of rotation after two orientation values are subtracted:

```
public float MapToRange (float rotation) {
    rotation %= 360.0f;
    if (Mathf.Abs(rotation) > 180.0f) {
        if (rotation < 0.0f)
            rotation += 360.0f;
        else
            rotation -= 360.0f;
    }
    return rotation;
}
```

3. Also, we need to create a basic behavior called `Align` that is the stepping stone for the facing algorithm. It uses the same principle as `Arrive`, but only in terms of rotation:

```
using UnityEngine;
using System.Collections;

public class Align : AgentBehaviour
{
    public float targetRadius;
    public float slowRadius;
    public float timeToTarget = 0.1f;

    public override Steering GetSteering()
    {
```

```
            Steering steering = new Steering();
            float targetOrientation = target.GetComponent<Agent>().
orientation;
            float rotation = targetOrientation - agent.orientation;
            rotation = MapToRange(rotation);
            float rotationSize = Mathf.Abs(rotation);
            if (rotationSize < targetRadius)
                return steering;
            float targetRotation;
            if (rotationSize > slowRadius)
                targetRotation = agent.maxRotation;
            else
                targetRotation = agent.maxRotation * rotationSize /
slowRadius;
            targetRotation *= rotation / rotationSize;
            steering.angular = targetRotation - agent.rotation;
            steering.angular /= timeToTarget;
            float angularAccel = Mathf.Abs(steering.angular);
            if (angularAccel > agent.maxAngularAccel)
            {
                steering.angular /= angularAccel;
                steering.angular *= agent.maxAngularAccel;
            }
            return steering;
        }
}
```

How to do it...

We now proceed to implement our facing algorithm that derives from `Align`:

1. Create the `Face` class along with a private auxiliary target member variable:

```
using UnityEngine;
using System.Collections;

public class Face : Align
{
    protected GameObject targetAux;
}
```

2. Override the `Awake` function to set up everything and swap references:

```
public override void Awake()
{
    base.Awake();
```

```
        targetAux = target;
        target = new GameObject();
        target.AddComponent<Agent>();
}
```

3. Also, implement the `OnDestroy` function to handle references and avoid memory issues:

```
void OnDestroy ()
{
    Destroy(target);
}
```

4. Finally, define the `GetSteering` function:

```
public override Steering GetSteering()
{
    Vector3 direction = targetAux.transform.position - transform.
position;
    if (direction.magnitude > 0.0f)
    {
        float targetOrientation = Mathf.Atan2(direction.x,
direction.z);
        targetOrientation *= Mathf.Rad2Deg;
        target.GetComponent<Agent>().orientation =
targetOrientation;
    }
    return base.GetSteering();
}
```

How it works...

The algorithm computes the internal target orientation according to the vector between the agent and the real target. Then, it just delegates the work to its parent class.

Wandering around

This technique works like a charm for random crowd simulations, animals, and almost any kind of NPC that requires random movement when idle.

Getting ready

We need to add another function to our `AgentBehaviour` class called `OriToVec` that converts an orientation value to a vector.

```
public Vector3 GetOriAsVec (float orientation) {
    Vector3 vector  = Vector3.zero;
    vector.x = Mathf.Sin(orientation * Mathf.Deg2Rad) * 1.0f;
    vector.z = Mathf.Cos(orientation * Mathf.Deg2Rad) * 1.0f;
    return vector.normalized;
}
```

How to do it...

We could see it as a big three-step process in which we manipulate the internal target position in a parameterized random way, face that position, and move accordingly:

1. Create the `Wander` class deriving from `Face`:

```
using UnityEngine;
using System.Collections;

public class Wander : Face
{
    public float offset;
    public float radius;
    public float rate;
}
```

2. Define the `Awake` function in order to set up the internal target:

```
public override void Awake()
{
    target = new GameObject();
    target.transform.position = transform.position;
    base.Awake();
}
```

3. Define the `GetSteering` function:

```
public override Steering GetSteering()
{
    Steering steering = new Steering();
    float wanderOrientation = Random.Range(-1.0f, 1.0f) * rate;
    float targetOrientation = wanderOrientation + agent.
orientation;
    Vector3 orientationVec = OriToVec(agent.orientation);
```

```
    Vector3 targetPosition = (offset * orientationVec) +
transform.position;
    targetPosition = targetPosition + (OriToVec(targetOrientation)
* radius);
    targetAux.transform.position = targetPosition;
    steering = base.GetSteering();
    steering.linear = targetAux.transform.position - transform.
position;
    steering.linear.Normalize();
    steering.linear *= agent.maxAccel;
    return steering;
}
```

How it works...

The behavior takes into consideration two radii in order to get a random position to go to next, looks towards that random point, and converts the computed orientation into a direction vector in order to advance.

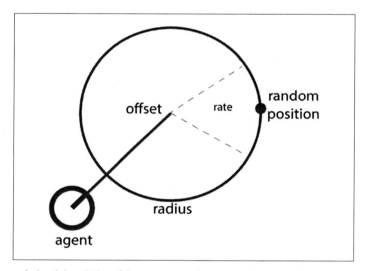

A visual description of the parameters for creating the Wander behavior

Following a path

There are times when we need scripted routes, and it's just inconceivable to do this entirely by code. Imagine you're working on a stealth game. Would you code a route for every single guard? This technique will help you build a flexible path system for those situations:

Getting ready

We need to define a custom data type called `PathSegment`:

```
using UnityEngine;
using System.Collections;

public class PathSegment
{
    public Vector3 a;
    public Vector3 b;

    public PathSegment () : this (Vector3.zero, Vector3.zero){}
    public PathSegment (Vector3 a, Vector3 b)
    {
        this.a = a;
        this.b = b;
    }
}
```

How to do it...

This is a long recipe that could be seen as a big two-step process. First, we build the `Path` class, which abstracts points in the path from their specific spatial representations, and then we build the `PathFollower` behavior, which makes use of that abstraction in order to get actual spatial points to follow:

1. Create the `Path` class, which consists of nodes and segments but only the nodes are public and assigned manually:

```
using UnityEngine;
using System.Collections;
using System.Collections.Generic;

public class Path : MonoBehaviour
{
    public List<GameObject> nodes;
    List<PathSegment> segments;
}
```

2. Define the `Start` function to set the segments when the scene starts:

```
void Start()
{
    segments = GetSegments();
}
```

3. Define the `GetSegments` function to build the segments from the nodes:

```
public List<PathSegment> GetSegments ()
{
    List<PathSegment> segments = new List<PathSegment>();
    int i;
    for (i = 0; i < nodes.Count - 1; i++)
    {
        Vector3 src = nodes[i].transform.position;
        Vector3 dst = nodes[i+1].transform.position;
        PathSegment segment = new PathSegment(src, dst);
        segments.Add(segment);
    }
    return segments;
}
```

4. Define the first function for abstraction, called `GetParam`:

```
public float GetParam(Vector3 position, float lastParam)
{
    // body
}
```

5. We need to find out which segment the agent is closest to:

```
float param = 0f;
PathSegment currentSegment = null;
float tempParam = 0f;
foreach (PathSegment ps in segments)
{
    tempParam += Vector3.Distance(ps.a, ps.b);
    if (lastParam <= tempParam)
    {
        currentSegment = ps;
        break;
    }
}
if (currentSegment == null)
    return 0f;
```

6. Given the current position, we need to work out the direction to go to:

```
Vector3 currPos = position - currentSegment.a;
Vector3 segmentDirection = currentSegment.b - currentSegment.a;
segmentDirection.Normalize();
```

7. Find the point in the segment using vector projection:

```
Vector3 pointInSegment = Vector3.Project(currPos,
segmentDirection);
```

8. Finally, GetParam returns the next position to go to along the path:

```
param = tempParam - Vector3.Distance(currentSegment.a,
currentSegment.b);
param += pointInSegment.magnitude;
return param;
```

9. Define the GetPosition function:

```
public Vector3 GetPosition(float param)
{
    // body
}
```

10. Given the current location along the path, we find the corresponding segment:

```
Vector3 position = Vector3.zero;
PathSegment currentSegment = null;
float tempParam = 0f;
foreach (PathSegment ps in segments)
{
    tempParam += Vector3.Distance(ps.a, ps.b);
    if (param <= tempParam)
    {
        currentSegment = ps;
        break;
    }
}
if (currentSegment == null)
    return Vector3.zero;
```

11. Finally, GetPosition converts the parameter as a spatial point and returns it:

```
Vector3 segmentDirection = currentSegment.b - currentSegment.a;
segmentDirection.Normalize();
tempParam -= Vector3.Distance(currentSegment.a, currentSegment.b);
tempParam = param - tempParam;
position = currentSegment.a + segmentDirection * tempParam;
return position;
```

12. Create the `PathFollower` behavior, which derives from `Seek` (remember to set the order of execution):

```
using UnityEngine;
using System.Collections;

public class PathFollower : Seek
{
    public Path path;
    public float pathOffset = 0.0f;
    float currentParam;
}
```

13. Implement the `Awake` function to set the target:

```
public override void Awake()
{
    base.Awake();
    target = new GameObject();
    currentParam = 0f;
}
```

14. The final step is to define the `GetSteering` function, which relies on the abstraction created by the `Path` class to set the target position and apply `Seek`:

```
public override Steering GetSteering()
{
    currentParam = path.GetParam(transform.position,
currentParam);
    float targetParam = currentParam + pathOffset;
    target.transform.position = path.GetPosition(targetParam);
    return base.GetSteering();
}
```

How it works...

We use the `Path` class in order to have a movement guideline. It is the cornerstone, because it relies on `GetParam` to map an offset point to follow in its internal guideline, and it also uses `GetPosition` to convert that referential point to a position in the three-dimensional space along the segments.

The path-following algorithm just makes use of the path's functions in order to get a new position, update the target, and apply the `Seek` behavior.

There's more...

It's important to take into account the order in which the nodes are linked in the Inspector for the path to work as expected. A practical way to achieve this is to manually name the nodes with a reference number.

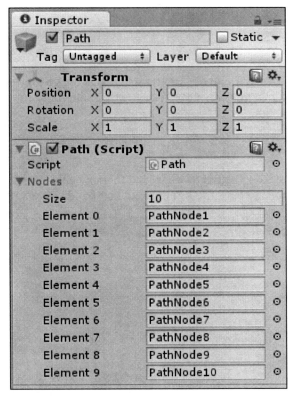

An example of a path set up in the Inspector window

Also, we could define the `OnDrawGizmos` function in order to have a better visual reference of the path:

```
void OnDrawGizmos ()
{
    Vector3 direction;
    Color tmp = Gizmos.color;
    Gizmos.color = Color.magenta;//example color
    int i;
    for (i = 0; i < nodes.Count - 1; i++)
    {
```

```
            Vector3 src = nodes[i].transform.position;
            Vector3 dst = nodes[i+1].transform.position;
            direction = dst - src;
            Gizmos.DrawRay(src, direction);
        }
        Gizmos.color = tmp;
    }
```

Avoiding agents

In crowd-simulation games, it would be unnatural to see agents behaving entirely like particles in a physics-based system. The goal of this recipe is to create an agent capable of mimicking our peer-evasion movement.

Getting ready

We need to create a tag called **Agent** and assign it to those game objects that we would like to avoid, and we also need to have the **Agent** script component attached to them.

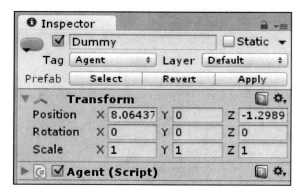

An example of how should look the Inspector of a dummy agent to avoid

How to do it...

This recipe will require the creation and handling of just one file:

1. Create the AvoidAgent behavior, which is composed of a collision avoidance radius and the list of agents to avoid:

```
using UnityEngine;
using System.Collections;
using System.Collections.Generic;

public class AvoidAgent : AgentBehaviour
```

```
{
    public float collisionRadius = 0.4f;
    GameObject[] targets;
}
```

2. Implement the `Start` function in order to set the list of agents according to the tag we created earlier:

```
void Start ()
{
    targets = GameObject.FindGameObjectsWithTag("Agent");
}
```

3. Define the `GetSteering` function:

```
public override Steering GetSteering()
{
    // body
}
```

4. Add the following variables to compute distances and velocities from agents that are nearby:

```
Steering steering = new Steering();
float shortestTime = Mathf.Infinity;
GameObject firstTarget = null;
float firstMinSeparation = 0.0f;
float firstDistance = 0.0f;
Vector3 firstRelativePos = Vector3.zero;
Vector3 firstRelativeVel = Vector3.zero;
```

5. Find the closest agent that is prone to collision with the current one:

```
foreach (GameObject t in targets)
{
    Vector3 relativePos;
    Agent targetAgent = t.GetComponent<Agent>();
    relativePos = t.transform.position - transform.position;
    Vector3 relativeVel = targetAgent.velocity - agent.velocity;
    float relativeSpeed = relativeVel.magnitude;
    float timeToCollision = Vector3.Dot(relativePos, relativeVel);
    timeToCollision /= relativeSpeed * relativeSpeed * -1;
    float distance = relativePos.magnitude;
    float minSeparation = distance - relativeSpeed *
timeToCollision;
    if (minSeparation > 2 * collisionRadius)
        continue;
    if (timeToCollision > 0.0f && timeToCollision < shortestTime)
    {
```

```
                    shortestTime = timeToCollision;
                    firstTarget = t;
                    firstMinSeparation = minSeparation;
                    firstRelativePos = relativePos;
                    firstRelativeVel = relativeVel;
                }
        }
```

6. If there is one, then get away:

```
if (firstTarget == null)
    return steering;
if (firstMinSeparation <= 0.0f || firstDistance < 2 *
collisionRadius)
    firstRelativePos = firstTarget.transform.position;
else
    firstRelativePos += firstRelativeVel * shortestTime;
firstRelativePos.Normalize();
steering.linear = -firstRelativePos * agent.maxAccel;
return steering;
```

How it works...

Given a list of agents, we take into consideration which one is closest, and if it is close enough, we make it so the agent tries to escape from the expected route of that first one according to its current velocity so that they don't collide.

There's more

This behavior works well when combined with other behaviors using blending techniques (some are included in this chapter); otherwise it's a starting point for your own collision avoidance algorithms.

Avoiding walls

This technique aims at imitating our capacity to evade walls by considering a safety margin, and creating repulsion from their surfaces when that gap is broken.

Getting ready

This technique uses the RaycastHit structure and the Raycast function from the physics engine, so it's recommended that you take a refresher on the docs in case you're a little rusty on the subject.

How to do it...

Thanks to our previous hard work, this recipe is a short one:

1. Create the `AvoidWall` behavior derived from `Seek`:

    ```
    using UnityEngine;
    using System.Collections;

    public class AvoidWall : Seek
    {
        // body
    }
    ```

2. Include the member variables for defining the safety margin, and the length of the ray to cast:

    ```
    public float avoidDistance;
    public float lookAhead;
    ```

3. Define the `Awake` function to set up the target:

    ```
    public override void Awake()
    {
        base.Awake();
        target = new GameObject();
    }
    ```

4. Define the `GetSteering` function for the following steps:

    ```
    public override Steering GetSteering()
    {
        // body
    }
    ```

5. Declare and set the variable needed for ray casting:

    ```
    Steering steering = new Steering();
    Vector3 position = transform.position;
    Vector3 rayVector = agent.velocity.normalized * lookAhead;
    Vector3 direction = rayVector;
    RaycastHit hit;
    ```

6. Cast the ray and make the proper calculations if a wall is hit:

    ```
    if (Physics.Raycast(position, direction, out hit, lookAhead))
    {
        position = hit.point + hit.normal * avoidDistance;
        target.transform.position = position;
        steering = base.GetSteering();
    }
    return steering;
    ```

How it works...

We cast a ray in front of the agent; when the ray collides with a wall, the target object is placed in a new position taking into consideration its distance from the wall and the safety distance declared and delegating the steering calculations to the Seek behavior; this creates the illusion of the agent avoiding the wall.

There's more...

We could extend this behavior by adding more rays, like whiskers, in order to get better accuracy. Also, it is usually paired with other movement behaviors, such as Pursue, using blending.

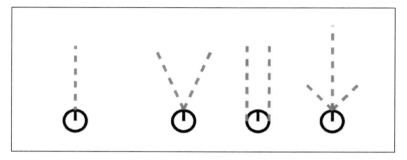

The original ray cast and possible extensions for more precise wall avoidance

See also

For further information on the RaycastHit structure and the Raycast function, please refer to the official documentation available online at:

- http://docs.unity3d.com/ScriptReference/RaycastHit.html
- http://docs.unity3d.com/ScriptReference/Physics.Raycast.html

Blending behaviors by weight

Blending techniques allow you to add behaviors and mix them without creating new scripts every time you need a new type of hybrid agent.

This is one of the most powerful techniques in this chapter, and it's probably the most used behaviour-blending approach because of its power and the low cost of implementation.

Getting ready

We must add a new member variable to our AgentBehaviour class called weight and preferably assign a default value—in this case, 1.0f. Besides this, we should refactor the Update function to incorporate weight as a parameter to the Agent class' SetSteering function. All in all, the new AgentBehaviour class should look something like this:

```
public class AgentBehaviour : MonoBehaviour
{
    public float weight = 1.0f;

    // ... the rest of the class

    public virtual void Update ()
    {
        agent.SetSteering(GetSteering(), weight);
    }
}
```

How to do it...

We just need to change the SetSteering agent function's signature and definition:

```
public void SetSteering (Steering steering, float weight)
{
    this.steering.linear += (weight * steering.linear);
    this.steering.angular += (weight * steering.angular);
}
```

How it works...

The weights are used to amplify the steering behavior result, and they're added to the main steering structure.

There's more...

The weights don't necessarily need to add up to 1.0f. The weight parameter is a reference for defining the relevance that the steering behavior will have among the other ones.

See also

In this project, there is an example of avoiding walls, worked out using weighted blending.

Blending behaviors by priority

Sometimes, weighted blending is not enough because heavyweight behaviors dilute the contributions of the lightweights, but those behaviors need to play their part too. That's when priority-based blending comes into play, applying a cascading effect from high-priority to low-priority behaviors.

Getting ready

The approach is very similar to the one used in the previous recipe. We must add a new member variable to our AgentBehaviour class. We should also refactor the Update function to incorporate priority as a parameter to the Agent class' SetSteering function. The new AgentBehaviour class should look something like this:

```
public class AgentBehaviour : MonoBehaviour
{
    public int priority = 1;
    // ... everything else stays the same
    public virtual void Update ()
    {
        agent.SetSteering(GetSteering(), priority);
    }
}
```

How to do it...

Now, we need to make some changes to the Agent class:

1. Add a new namespace from the library:

    ```
    using System.Collections.Generic;
    ```

2. Add the member variable for the minimum steering value to consider a group of behaviors:

    ```
    public float priorityThreshold = 0.2f;
    ```

3. Add the member variable for holding the group of behavior results:

    ```
    private Dictionary<int, List<Steering>> groups;
    ```

4. Initialize the variable in the Start function:

    ```
    groups = new Dictionary<int, List<Steering>>();
    ```

5. Modify the `LateUpdate` function so that the steering variable is set by calling `GetPrioritySteering`:

```
public virtual void LateUpdate ()
{
    //  funnelled steering through priorities
    steering = GetPrioritySteering();
    groups.Clear();
    // ... the rest of the computations stay the same
    steering = new Steering();
}
```

6. Modify the `SetSteering` function's signature and definition to store the steering values in their corresponding priority groups:

```
public void SetSteering (Steering steering, int priority)
{
    if (!groups.ContainsKey(priority))
    {
        groups.Add(priority, new List<Steering>());
    }
    groups[priority].Add(steering);
}
```

7. Finally, implement the `GetPrioritySteering` function to funnel the steering group:

```
private Steering GetPrioritySteering ()
{
    Steering steering = new Steering();
    float sqrThreshold = priorityThreshold * priorityThreshold;
    foreach (List<Steering> group in groups.Values)
    {
        steering = new Steering();
        foreach (Steering singleSteering in group)
        {
            steering.linear += singleSteering.linear;
            steering.angular += singleSteering.angular;
        }
        if (steering.linear.sqrMagnitude > sqrThreshold ||
                Mathf.Abs(steering.angular) > priorityThreshold)
        {
            return steering;
        }
    }
}
```

How it works...

By creating priority groups, we blend behaviors that are common to one another, and the first group in which the steering value exceeds the threshold is selected. Otherwise, steering from the least-priority group is chosen.

There's more...

We could extend this approach by mixing it with weighted blending; in this way, we would have a more robust architecture by getting extra precision on the way the behaviors make an impact on the agent in every priority level:

```
foreach (Steering singleSteering in group)
{
    steering.linear += singleSteering.linear * weight;
    steering.angular += singleSteering.angular * weight;
}
```

See also

There is an example of avoiding walls using priority-based blending in this project.

Combining behaviors using a steering pipeline

This is a different approach to creating and blending behaviors that is based on goals. It tries to be a middle-ground between movement-blending and planning, without the implementation costs of the latter.

Getting ready

Using a steering pipeline slightly changes the train of thought used so far. We need to think in terms of goals, and constraints. That said, the heavy lifting rests on the base classes and the derived classes that will define the behaviors; we need to start by implementing them.

The following code is for the `Targeter` class. It can be seen as a goal-driven behavior:

```
using UnityEngine;
using System.Collections;

public class Targeter : MonoBehaviour
{
    public virtual Goal GetGoal()
```

```
    {
        return new Goal();
    }
}
```

Now, we create the Decomposer class:

```
using UnityEngine;
using System.Collections;

public class Decomposer : MonoBehaviour
{
    public virtual Goal Decompose (Goal goal)
    {
        return goal;
    }
}
```

We also need a Constraint class:

```
using UnityEngine;
using System.Collections;

public class Constraint : MonoBehaviour
{
    public virtual bool WillViolate (Path path)
    {
        return true;
    }

    public virtual Goal Suggest (Path path) {
        return new Goal();
    }
}
```

And finally, an Actuator class:

```
using UnityEngine;
using System.Collections;

public class Actuator : MonoBehaviour
{
    public virtual Path GetPath (Goal goal)
    {
        return new Path();
```

```
        }

        public virtual Steering GetOutput (Path path, Goal goal)
        {
            return new Steering();
        }
    }
```

How to do it...

The `SteeringPipeline` class makes use of the previously implemented classes in order to work, maintaining the component-driven pipeline but with a different approach, as mentioned earlier:

1. Create the `SteeringPipeline` class deriving from the `Wander` behavior, including the array of components that it handles:

    ```
    using UnityEngine;
    using System.Collections;
    using System.Collections.Generic;

    public class SteeringPipeline : Wander
    {
        public int constraintSteps = 3;
        Targeter[] targeters;
        Decomposer[] decomposers;
        Constraint[] constraints;
        Actuator actuator;
    }
    ```

2. Define the `Start` function to set the references to the attached components in the game object:

    ```
    void Start ()
    {
        targeters = GetComponents<Targeter>();
        decomposers = GetComponents<Decomposer>();
        constraints = GetComponents<Constraint>();
        actuator = GetComponent<Actuator>();
    }
    ```

3. Define the `GetSteering` function to work out the goal and the steering value to reach it:

    ```
    public override Steering GetSteering()
    {
        Goal goal = new Goal();
    ```

```
foreach (Targeter targeter in targeters)
    goal.UpdateChannels(targeter.GetGoal());
foreach (Decomposer decomposer in decomposers)
    goal = decomposer.Decompose(goal);
for (int i = 0; i < constraintSteps; i++)
{
    Path path = actuator.GetPath(goal);
    foreach (Constraint constraint in constraints)
    {
        if (constraint.WillViolate(path))
        {
            goal = constraint.Suggest(path);
            break;
        }
        return actuator.GetOutput(path, goal);
    }
}
return base.GetSteering();
}
```

How it works...

This code takes a composite goal generated by *targeters*, creates sub-goals using *decomposers*, and evaluates them to comply with defined *constraints* before "blending" them into a final goal in order to produce a steering result. If everything fails (the constraints are not satisfied), it uses the default `Wander` behavior.

There's more...

You should try to implement some of the behavior recipes in terms of targeters, decomposers, constraints, and an actuator. Take into account that there's room for one actuator only, and it's the one responsible for making the final decision. A good example is as follows:

- **Targeters**: seeking, arriving, facing, and matching velocity
- **Decomposers**: path-finding algorithms
- **Constraints**: avoiding walls/agents

See also

For more theoretical insights, refer to Ian Millington's book, *Artificial Intelligence for Games*.

Shooting a projectile

This is the stepping stone for scenarios where we want to have control over gravity-reliant objects, such as balls and grenades, so we can then predict the projectile's landing spot, or be able to effectively shoot a projectile at a given target.

Getting ready

This recipe differs slightly as it doesn't rely on the base `AgentBehaviour` class.

How to do it...

1. Create the `Projectile` class along with its member variables to handle the physics:

```csharp
using UnityEngine;
using System.Collections;

public class Projectile : MonoBehaviour
{
    private bool set = false;
    private Vector3 firePos;
    private Vector3 direction;
    private float speed;
    private float timeElapsed;
}
```

2. Define the `Update` function:

```csharp
void Update ()
{
    if (!set)
        return;
    timeElapsed += Time.deltaTime;
    transform.position = firePos + direction * speed *
timeElapsed;
    transform.position += Physics.gravity * (timeElapsed *
timeElapsed) / 2.0f;
    // extra validation for cleaning the scene
    if (transform.position.y < -1.0f)
        Destroy(this.gameObject);// or set = false; and hide it
}
```

3. Finally, implement the `Set` function in order to fire the game object (for example, calling it after it is instantiated in the scene):

```
public void Set (Vector3 firePos, Vector3 direction, float speed)
{
    this.firePos = firePos;
    this.direction = direction.normalized;
    this.speed = speed;
    transform.position = firePos;
    set = true;
}
```

How it works...

This behavior uses high-school physics in order to generate the parabolic movement.

There's more...

We could also take another approach: implementing public properties in the script or declaring member variables as public and, instead of calling the `Set` function, having the script disabled by default in the prefab and enabling it after all the properties have been set. That way, we could easily apply the object pool pattern.

See also

For further information on the object pool pattern, please refer to the following Wikipedia article and an official Unity Technologies video tutorial available online at the following addresses:

- `http://en.wikipedia.org/wiki/Object_pool_pattern`
- `http://unity3d.com/learn/tutorials/modules/beginner/live-training-archive/object-pooling`

Predicting a projectile's landing spot

After a projectile is shot, some agents need to make a run for it, if we're talking about a grenade, or look at it when we're developing a sports game. In either case, it's important to predict the projectile's landing spot in order to make decisions:

Getting ready

Before we get into predicting the landing position, it's important to know the time left before it hits the ground (or reaches a certain position). Thus, instead of creating new behaviors, we need to update the `Projectile` class.

How to do it...

1. First, we need to add the `GetLandingTime` function to compute the landing time:

```
public float GetLandingTime (float height = 0.0f)
{
    Vector3 position = transform.position;
    float time = 0.0f;
    float valueInt = (direction.y * direction.y) * (speed *
speed);
    valueInt = valueInt - (Physics.gravity.y * 2 * (position.y -
height));
    valueInt = Mathf.Sqrt(valueInt);
    float valueAdd = (-direction.y) * speed;
    float valueSub = (-direction.y) * speed;
    valueAdd = (valueAdd + valueInt) / Physics.gravity.y;
    valueSub = (valueSub - valueInt) / Physics.gravity.y;
    if (float.IsNaN(valueAdd) && !float.IsNaN(valueSub))
        return valueSub;
    else if (!float.IsNaN(valueAdd) && float.IsNaN(valueSub))
        return valueAdd;
    else if (float.IsNaN(valueAdd) && float.IsNaN(valueSub))
        return -1.0f;
    time = Mathf.Max(valueAdd, valueSub);
    return time;
}
```

2. Now, we add the `GetLandingPos` function to predict the landing spot:

```
public Vector3 GetLandingPos (float height = 0.0f)
{
    Vector3 landingPos = Vector3.zero;
    float time = GetLandingTime();
    if (time < 0.0f)
        return landingPos;
    landingPos.y = height;
    landingPos.x = firePos.x + direction.x * speed * time;
    landingPos.z = firePos.z + direction.z * speed * time;
    return landingPos;
}
```

How it works...

First, we solve the equation from the previous recipe for a fixed height and, given the projectile's current position and speed, we are able to get the time at which the projectile will reach the given height.

There's more...

Take into account the NaN validation. It's placed that way because there may be two, one, or no solution to the equation. Furthermore, when the landing time is less than zero, it means the projectile won't be able to reach the target height.

Targeting a projectile

Just like it's important to predict a projectile's landing point, it's also important to develop intelligent agents capable of aiming projectiles. It wouldn't be fun if our rugby-player agents aren't capable of passing the ball.

Getting ready

Just like the previous recipe, we only need to expand the Projectile class.

How to do it...

Thanks to our previous hard work, this recipe is a real piece of cake:

1. Create the GetFireDirection function:

```
public static Vector3 GetFireDirection (Vector3 startPos, Vector3
endPos, float speed)
{
    // body
}
```

2. Solve the corresponding quadratic equation:

```
Vector3 direction = Vector3.zero;
Vector3 delta = endPos - startPos;
float a = Vector3.Dot(Physics.gravity, Physics.gravity);
float b = -4 * (Vector3.Dot(Physics.gravity, delta) + speed *
speed);
float c = 4 * Vector3.Dot(delta, delta);
if (4 * a * c > b * b)
    return direction;
```

```
float time0 = Mathf.Sqrt((-b + Mathf.Sqrt(b * b - 4 * a * c)) /
(2*a));
float time1 = Mathf.Sqrt((-b - Mathf.Sqrt(b * b - 4 * a * c)) /
(2*a));
```

3. If shooting the projectile is feasible given the parameters, return a non-zero direction vector:

```
float time;
if (time0 < 0.0f)
{
    if (time1 < 0)
        return direction;
    time = time1;
}
else
{
    if (time1 < 0)
        time = time0;
    else
        time = Mathf.Min(time0, time1);
}
direction = 2 * delta - Physics.gravity * (time * time);
direction = direction / (2 * speed * time);
return direction;
```

How it works...

Given a fixed speed, we solve the corresponding quadratic equation in order to obtain the desired direction (when at least one time value is available), which doesn't need to be normalized because we already normalized the vector while setting up the projectile.

There's more...

Take into account that we are returning a *blank* direction when time is negative; it means that the speed is not sufficient. One way to overcome this is to define a function that tests different speeds and then shoots the projectile.

Another relevant improvement is to add an extra parameter of the type `bool` for those cases when we have two valid times (which means two possible arcs), and we need to shoot over an obstacle such as a wall:

```
if (isWall)
    time = Mathf.Max(time0, time1);
else
    time = Mathf.Min(time0, time1);
```

Creating a jump system

Imagine that we're developing a cool action game where the player is capable of escaping using cliffs and rooftops. In that case, the enemies need to be able to chase the player and be smart enough to discern whether to take the jump and gauge how to do it.

Getting ready

We need to create a basic matching-velocity algorithm and the notion of jump pads and landing pads in order to emulate a velocity math so that we can reach them.

Also, the agents must have the tag `Agent`, the main object must have a `Collider` component marked as trigger. Depending on your game, the agent or the pads will need the `Rigidbody` component attached.

The following is the code for the `VelocityMatch` behavior:

```
using UnityEngine;
using System.Collections;

public class VelocityMatch : AgentBehaviour {

    public float timeToTarget = 0.1f;

    public override Steering GetSteering()
    {
        Steering steering = new Steering();
        steering.linear = target.GetComponent<Agent>().velocity -
agent.velocity;
        steering.linear /= timeToTarget;
        if (steering.linear.magnitude > agent.maxAccel)
            steering.linear = steering.linear.normalized * agent.
maxAccel;

        steering.angular = 0.0f;
        return steering;
    }
}
```

Also, it's important to create a data type called `JumpPoint`:

```
using UnityEngine;

public class JumpPoint
{
```

```
    public Vector3 jumpLocation;
    public Vector3 landingLocation;
    //The change in position from jump to landing
    public Vector3 deltaPosition;

    public JumpPoint ()
        : this (Vector3.zero, Vector3.zero)
    {
    }

    public JumpPoint(Vector3 a, Vector3 b)
    {
        this.jumpLocation = a;
        this.landingLocation = b;
        this.deltaPosition = this.landingLocation - this.jumpLocation;
    }
}
```

How to do it...

We will learn how to implement the Jump behavior:

1. Create the Jump class deriving from VelocityMatch, with its member variables:

```
using UnityEngine;
using System.Collections.Generic;

public class Jump : VelocityMatch
{
    public JumpPoint jumpPoint;
    //Keeps track of whether the jump is achievable
    bool canAchieve = false;
    //Holds the maximum vertical jump velocity
    public float maxYVelocity;
    public Vector3 gravity = new Vector3(0, -9.8f, 0);
    private Projectile projectile;
    private List<AgentBehaviour> behaviours;

    // next steps
}
```

2. Implement the `Isolate` method. It disables all the agent behaviors, except for the `Jump` component:

```
public void Isolate(bool state)
{
    foreach (AgentBehaviour b in behaviours)
        b.enabled = !state;
    this.enabled = state;
}
```

3. Define the function for calling the jumping effect, using the projectile behavior we learned before:

```
public void DoJump()
{
    projectile.enabled = true;
    Vector3 direction;
    direction = Projectile.GetFireDirection(jumpPoint.
jumpLocation, jumpPoint.landingLocation, agent.maxSpeed);
    projectile.Set(jumpPoint.jumpLocation, direction, agent.
maxSpeed, false);
}
```

4. Implement the member function for setting up the behaviors' target for matching its velocity:

```
protected void CalculateTarget()
{
    target = new GameObject();
    target.AddComponent<Agent>();

    //Calculate the first jump time
    float sqrtTerm = Mathf.Sqrt(2f * gravity.y * jumpPoint.
deltaPosition.y + maxYVelocity * agent.maxSpeed);
    float time = (maxYVelocity - sqrtTerm) / gravity.y;

    //Check if we can use it, otherwise try the other time
    if (!CheckJumpTime(time))
    {
        time = (maxYVelocity + sqrtTerm) / gravity.y;
    }
}
```

5. Implement the function for computing the time:

```
//Private helper method for the CalculateTarget function
private bool CheckJumpTime(float time)
{
    //Calculate the planar speed
    float vx = jumpPoint.deltaPosition.x / time;
    float vz = jumpPoint.deltaPosition.z / time;
    float speedSq = vx * vx + vz * vz;

    //Check it to see if we have a valid solution
    if (speedSq < agent.maxSpeed * agent.maxSpeed)
    {
        target.GetComponent<Agent>().velocity = new Vector3(vx,
0f, vz);
        canAchieve = true;
        return true;
    }
    return false;
}
```

6. Override the `Awake` member function. The most important thing here is caching the references to other attached behaviors, so `Isolate` function makes sense:

```
public override void Awake()
{
    base.Awake();
    this.enabled = false;
    projectile = gameObject.AddComponent<Projectile>();
    behaviours = new List<AgentBehaviour>();
    AgentBehaviour[] abs;
    abs = gameObject.GetComponents<AgentBehaviour>();
    foreach (AgentBehaviour b in abs)
    {
        if (b == this)
            continue;
        behaviours.Add(b);
    }
}
```

7. Override the `GetSteering` member function:

```
public override Steering GetSteering()
{
    Steering steering = new Steering();

    // Check if we have a trajectory, and create one if not.
    if (jumpPoint != null && target == null)
    {
        CalculateTarget();
    }
    //Check if the trajectory is zero. If not, we have no
acceleration.
    if (!canAchieve)
    {
        return steering;
    }

    //Check if we've hit the jump point
    if (Mathf.Approximately((transform.position - target.
transform.position).magnitude, 0f) &&
        Mathf.Approximately((agent.velocity - target.
GetComponent<Agent>().velocity).magnitude, 0f))
    {
        DoJump();
        return steering;
    }
    return base.GetSteering();
}
```

How it works...

The algorithm takes into account the agent's velocity and calculates whether it can reach the landing pad or not. The behavior's target is the one responsible for executing the jump, and if it judges that the agent can, it tries to match the targets' vertical velocity while seeking the landing pad's position.

There is more

We will need a jump pad and a landing pad in order to have a complete jumping system. Both the jump and landing pads need the `Collider` component marked as trigger. Also, as stated before, they will probably need to have a `Rigidbody` component, too, as seen in the image below.

The pads we will need a `MonoBehaviour` script attached as explained below.

The following code is to be attached to the jump pad:

```
using UnityEngine;

public class JumpLocation : MonoBehaviour
{
    public LandingLocation landingLocation;

    public void OnTriggerEnter(Collider other)
    {
        if (!other.gameObject.CompareTag("Agent"))
            return;
```

```
            Agent agent = other.GetComponent<Agent>();
            Jump jump = other.GetComponent<Jump>();
            if (agent == null || jump == null)
                return;
            Vector3 originPos = transform.position;
            Vector3 targetPos = landingLocation.transform.position;
            jump.Isolate(true);
            jump.jumpPoint = new JumpPoint(originPos, targetPos);
            jump.DoJump();
        }
    }
```

The following code is to be attached to the landing pad:

```
    using UnityEngine;

    public class LandingLocation : MonoBehaviour
    {
        public void OnTriggerEnter(Collider other)
        {
            if (!other.gameObject.CompareTag("Agent"))
                return;
            Agent agent = other.GetComponent<Agent>();
            Jump jump = other.GetComponent<Jump>();
            if (agent == null || jump == null)
                return;
            jump.Isolate(false);
            jump.jumpPoint = null;
        }
    }
```

See Also

The *Shooting a projectile* recipe

2
Navigation

In this chapter, we will cover the following recipes:

- ▶ Representing the world with grids
- ▶ Representing the world with Dirichlet domains
- ▶ Representing the world with points of visibility
- ▶ Representing the world with a self-made navigation mesh
- ▶ Finding your way out of a maze with DFS
- ▶ Finding the shortest path in a grid with BFS
- ▶ Finding the shortest path with Dijkstra
- ▶ Finding the best-promising path with A*
- ▶ Improving A* for memory: IDA*
- ▶ Planning navigation in several frames: time-sliced search
- ▶ Smoothing a path

Introduction

In this chapter, we will learn path-finding algorithms for navigating complex scenarios. Game worlds are usually complex structures; whether a maze, an open world, or everything in between. That's why we need different techniques for approaching these kinds of problems.

We'll learn some ways of representing the world using different kinds of graph structures, and several algorithms for finding a path, each aimed at different situations.

It is worth mentioning that path-finding algorithms rely on techniques such as `Seek` and `Arrive`, learnt in the previous chapter, in order to navigate the map.

Representing the world with grids

A grid is the most used structure for representing worlds in games because it is easy to implement and visualize. However, we will lay the foundations for advanced graph representations while learning the basis of graph theory and properties.

Getting ready

First, we need to create an abstract class called `Graph`, declaring the virtual methods that every graph representation implements. It is done this way because, no matter how the vertices and edges are represented internally, the path-finding algorithms remain high-level, thus avoiding the implementation of the algorithms for each type of graph representation.

This class works as a parent class for the different representations to be learned in the chapter and it's a good starting point if you want to implement graph representations not covered in the book.

The following is the code for the `Graph` class:

1. Create the backbone with the member values:

```
using UnityEngine;
using System.Collections;
using System.Collections.Generic;

public abstract class Graph : MonoBehaviour
{
    public GameObject vertexPrefab;
    protected List<Vertex> vertices;
    protected List<List<Vertex>> neighbours;
    protected List<List<float>> costs;
    // next steps
}
```

2. Define the Start function:

```
public virtual void Start()
{
    Load();
}
```

3. Define the Load function, mentioned previously:

```
public virtual void Load() { }
```

4. Implement the function for getting the graph's size:

```
public virtual int GetSize()
{
    if (ReferenceEquals(vertices, null))
        return 0;
    return vertices.Count;
}
```

5. Define the function for finding the nearest vertex given a position:

```
public virtual Vertex GetNearestVertex(Vector3 position)
{
    return null;
}
```

6. Implement the function for getting the vertex given its ID:

```
public virtual Vertex GetVertexObj(int id)
{
    if (ReferenceEquals(vertices, null) || vertices.Count == 0)
        return null;
    if (id < 0 || id >= vertices.Count)
        return null;
    return vertices[id];
}
```

7. Implement the function for retrieving a vertex' neighbours:

```
public virtual Vertex[] GetNeighbours(Vertex v)
{
    if (ReferenceEquals(neighbours, null) || neighbours.Count ==
0)
        return new Vertex[0];
    if (v.id < 0 || v.id >= neighbours.Count)
        return new Vertex[0];
    return neighbours[v.id].ToArray();
}
```

We also need a `Vertex` class, with the following code:

```
using UnityEngine;
using System.Collections.Generic;
[System.Serializable]
public class Vertex : MonoBehaviour
{
    public int id;
    public List<Edge> neighbours;
    [HideInInspector]
    public Vertex prev;
}
```

Following, we need to create a class for storing a vertex' neighbours with their costs. This class will be called `Edge`, and let's implement it:

1. Create the `Edge` class, deriving from `IComparable`:

```
using System;

[System.Serializable]
public class Edge : IComparable<Edge>
{
    public float cost;
    public Vertex vertex;
    // next steps
}
```

2. Implement its constructor:

```
public Edge(Vertex vertex = null, float cost = 1f)
{
    this.vertex = vertex;
    this.cost = cost;
}
```

3. Implement the comparison member function:

```
public int CompareTo(Edge other)
{
    float result = cost - other.cost;
    int idA = vertex.GetInstanceID();
    int idB = other.vertex.GetInstanceID();
    if (idA == idB)
        return 0;
    return (int)result;
}
```

4. Implement the function for comparing two edges:

```
public bool Equals(Edge other)
{
    return (other.vertex.id == this.vertex.id);
}
```

5. Override the function for comparing two objects:

```
public override bool Equals(object obj)
{
    Edge other = (Edge)obj;
    return (other.vertex.id == this.vertex.id);
}
```

6. Override the function for retrieving the hash code. This is necessary when overriding the previous member function:

```
public override int GetHashCode()
{
    return this.vertex.GetHashCode();
}
```

Besides creating the previous classes, it's important to define a couple of prefabs based on the cube primitive in order to visualize the ground (maybe a low-height cube) and walls or obstacles. The prefab for the ground is assigned to the `vertexPrefab` variable and the wall prefab is assigned to the `obstaclePrefab` variable that is declared in the next section.

Finally, create a directory called `Maps` to store the text files for defining the maps.

How to do it...

Now, it's time to go in-depth and be concrete about implementing our grid graph. First, we implement all the functions for handling the graph, leaving space for your own text files, and in a following section we'll learn how to read `.map` files, which is an open format used by a lot of games:

1. Create the `GraphGrid` class deriving from Graph

```
using UnityEngine;
using System;
using System.Collections.Generic;
using System.IO;

public class GraphGrid : Graph
{
    public GameObject obstaclePrefab;
    public string mapName = "arena.map";
    public bool get8Vicinity = false;
    public float cellSize = 1f;
    [Range(0, Mathf.Infinity)]
    public float defaultCost = 1f;
    [Range(0, Mathf.Infinity)]
    public float maximumCost = Mathf.Infinity;
    string mapsDir = "Maps";
    int numCols;
    int numRows;
    GameObject[] vertexObjs;
    // this is necessary for
    // the advanced section of reading
```

```
            // from an example test file
            bool[,] mapVertices;
            // next steps
    }
```

2. Define the `GridToId` and `IdToGrid` functions for transforming a position in the grid into a vertex index, and vice versa, respectively

```
private int GridToId(int x, int y)
{
    return Math.Max(numRows, numCols) * y + x;
}

private Vector2 IdToGrid(int id)
{
    Vector2 location = Vector2.zero;
    location.y = Mathf.Floor(id / numCols);
    location.x = Mathf.Floor(id % numCols);
    return location;
}
```

3. Define the `LoadMap` function for reading the text file:

```
private void LoadMap(string filename)
{
    // TODO
    // implement your grid-based
    // file-reading procedure here
    // using
    // vertices[i, j] for logical representation and
    // vertexObjs[i, j] for assigning new prefab instances
}
```

4. Override the LoadGraph function:

```
public override void LoadGraph()
{
    LoadMap(mapName);
}
```

5. Override the `GetNearestVertex` function. This is the traditional way, without considering that the resulting vertex is an obstacle. In the next steps we will learn how to do it better:

```
public override Vertex GetNearestVertex(Vector3 position)
{
    position.x = Mathf.Floor(position.x / cellSize);
    position.y = Mathf.Floor(position.z / cellSize);
```

```
        int col = (int)position.x;
        int row = (int)position.z;
        int id = GridToId(col, row);
        return vertices[id];
    }
```

6. Override the `GetNearestVertex` function. It's is based on the Breadth-First Search algorithm that we will learn in depth later in the chapter:

```
public override Vertex GetNearestVertex(Vector3 position)
{
    int col = (int)(position.x / cellSize);
    int row = (int)(position.z / cellSize);
    Vector2 p = new Vector2(col, row);
    // next steps
}
```

7. Define the list of explored positions (vertices) and the queue of position to be explored:

```
List<Vector2> explored = new List<Vector2>();
Queue<Vector2> queue = new Queue<Vector2>();
queue.Enqueue(p);
```

8. Do it while the queue still have elements to explore. Otherwise, return null:

```
do
{
    p = queue.Dequeue();
    col = (int)p.x;
    row = (int)p.y;
    int id = GridToId(col, row);
    // next steps
} while (queue.Count != 0);
return null;
```

9. Retrieve it immediately if it's a valid vertex:

```
if (mapVertices[row, col])
    return vertices[id];
```

10. Add the position to the list of explored, if it's not already there:

```
if (!explored.Contains(p))
{
    explored.Add(p);
    int i, j;
    // next step
}
```

11. Add all its valid neighbors to the queue, provided they're valid:

```
for (i = row - 1; i <= row + 1; i++)
{
    for (j = col - 1; j <= col + 1; j++)
    {
        if (i < 0 || j < 0)
            continue;
        if (j >= numCols || i >= numRows)
            continue;
        if (i == row && j == col)
            continue;
        queue.Enqueue(new Vector2(j, i));
    }
}
```

How it works...

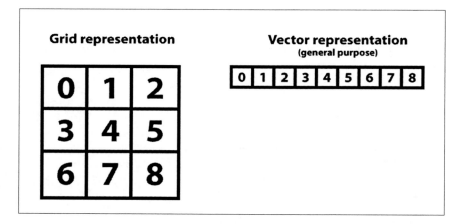

The algorithm makes use of its private functions in order to adapt itself to the general functions derived from the parent's class, and it relies on simple mathematical functions to convert from a two-dimensional vector position to a one-dimensional vector, or vertex index.

The LoadMap function is open to your own implementation, but in the next section we we'll learn a way to implement and read certain kinds of text files containing maps based on grids.

There's more...

We'll learn a way to implement the LoadMap function by using the .map file format as an example:

1. Define the function and create a StreamReader object for reading the file

```
private void LoadMap(string filename)
{
    string path = Application.dataPath + "/" + mapsDir + "/" +
filename;
    try
    {
        StreamReader strmRdr = new StreamReader(path);
        using (strmRdr)
        {
            // next steps in here
        }
    }
    catch (Exception e)
    {
        Debug.LogException(e);
    }
}
```

2. Declare and initialize the necessary variables

```
int j = 0;
int i = 0;
int id = 0;
string line;
Vector3 position = Vector3.zero;
Vector3 scale = Vector3.zero;
```

3. Read the header of the file containing its height and width

```
line = strmRdr.ReadLine();// non-important line
line = strmRdr.ReadLine();// height
numRows = int.Parse(line.Split(' ')[1]);
line = strmRdr.ReadLine();// width
numCols = int.Parse(line.Split(' ')[1]);
line = strmRdr.ReadLine();// "map" line in file
```

4. Initialize the member variables, allocating memory at the same time:

```
vertices = new List<Vertex>(numRows * numCols);
neighbours = new List<List<Vertex>>(numRows * numCols);
costs = new List<List<float>>(numRows * numCols);
vertexObjs = new GameObject[numRows * numCols];
    mapVertices = new bool[numRows, numCols];
```

5. Declare the for loop for iterating over the characters in the following lines

```
for (i = 0; i < numRows; i++)
{
    line = strmRdr.ReadLine();
    for (j = 0; j < numCols; j++)
    {
        // next steps in here
    }
}
```

6. Assign true or false to the logical representation depending on the character read

```
bool isGround = true;
if (line[j] != '.')
    isGround = false;
mapVertices[i, j] = isGround;
```

7. Instantiate the proper prefab

```
position.x = j * cellSize;
position.z = i * cellSize;
id = GridToId(j, i);
if (isGround)
    vertexObjs[id] = Instantiate(vertexPrefab, position,
Quaternion.identity) as GameObject;
else
    vertexObjs[id] = Instantiate(obstaclePrefab, position,
Quaternion.identity) as GameObject;
```

8. Assign the new game object as a child of the graph and clean-up its name

```
vertexObjs[id].name = vertexObjs[id].name.Replace("(Clone)",
id.ToString());
Vertex v = vertexObjs[id].AddComponent<Vertex>();
v.id = id;
vertices.Add(v);
neighbours.Add(new List<Vertex>());
costs.Add(new List<float>());
float y = vertexObjs[id].transform.localScale.y;
```

```
scale = new Vector3(cellSize, y, cellSize);
vertexObjs[id].transform.localScale = scale;
vertexObjs[id].transform.parent = gameObject.transform;
```

9. Create a pair of nested loops right after the previous loop, for setting up the neighbors for each vertex:

```
for (i = 0; i < numRows; i++)
{
    for (j = 0; j < numCols; j++)
    {
        SetNeighbours(j, i);
    }
}
```

10. Define the SetNeighbours function, called in the previous step:

```
protected void SetNeighbours(int x, int y, bool get8 = false)
{
    int col = x;
    int row = y;
    int i, j;
    int vertexId = GridToId(x, y);
    neighbours[vertexId] = new List<Vertex>();
    costs[vertexId] = new List<float>();
    Vector2[] pos = new Vector2[0];
    // next steps
}
```

11. Compute the proper values when we need vicinity of eight (top, bottom, right, left, and corners):

```
if (get8)
{
    pos = new Vector2[8];
    int c = 0;
    for (i = row - 1; i <= row + 1; i++)
    {
        for (j = col -1; j <= col; j++)
        {
            pos[c] = new Vector2(j, i);
            c++;
        }
    }
}
```

12. Set up everything for vicinity of four (no corners):

```
else
{
    pos = new Vector2[4];
    pos[0] = new Vector2(col, row - 1);
    pos[1] = new Vector2(col - 1, row);
    pos[2] = new Vector2(col + 1, row);
    pos[3] = new Vector2(col, row + 1);
}
```

13. Add the neighbors in the lists. It's the same procedure regarding the type of vicinity:

```
foreach (Vector2 p in pos)
{
    i = (int)p.y;
    j = (int)p.x;
    if (i < 0 || j < 0)
        continue;
    if (i >= numRows || j >= numCols)
        continue;
    if (i == row && j == col)
        continue;
    if (!mapVertices[i, j])
        continue;
    int id = GridToId(j, i);
    neighbours[vertexId].Add(vertices[id]);
    costs[vertexId].Add(defaultCost);
}
```

See also

For further information about the map's format used and getting free maps from several acclaimed titles, please refer to the *Moving AI Lab's* website, led by Professor Sturtevant, available online at http://movingai.com/benchmarks/

Representing the world with Dirichlet domains

Also called a Voronoi polygon, a Dirichlet domain is a way of dividing space into regions consisting of a set of points closer to a given seed point than to any other. This graph representation helps in distributing the space using Unity's primitives or existing meshes, thus not really adhering to the definition, but using the concept as a means to an end. Dirichlet domains are usually mapped using cones for delimiting the area of a given vertex, but we're adapting that principle to our specific needs and tool.

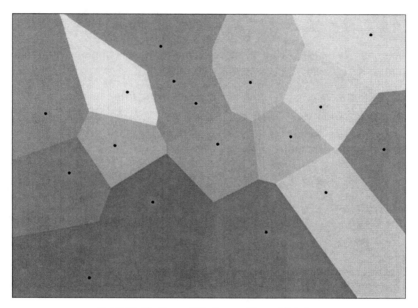

Example of a Voronoi Diagram or Voronoi Polygon

Getting ready

Before building our new `Graph` class, it's important to create the `VertexReport` class, make some modifications to our `Graph` class, and add the `Vertex` tag in the project:

1. Prepend the `VertexReport` class to the `Graph` class specification, in the same file:

```
public class VertexReport
{
    public int vertex;
    public GameObject obj;
    public VertexReport(int vertexId, GameObject obj)
    {
```

```
                    vertex = vertexId;
                    this.obj = obj;
            }
    }
```

 It's worth noting that the vertex objects in the scene must have a collider component attached to them, as well as the Vertex tag assigned. These objects can be either primitives or meshes, covering the maximum size of the area to be considered that vertex node.

How to do it...

This can be seen as a two-step recipe. First we define the vertex implementation and then the graph implementation, so everything works as intended:

1. First, create the VertexDirichlet class deriving from Vertex:

    ```
    using UnityEngine;

    public class VertexDirichlet : Vertex
    {
        // next steps
    }
    ```

2. Define the OnTriggerEnter function for registering the object in the current vertex:

    ```
    public void OnTriggerEnter(Collider col)
    {
        string objName = col.gameObject.name;
        if (objName.Equals("Agent") || objName.Equals("Player"))
        {
            VertexReport report = new VertexReport(id, col.
    gameObject);
            SendMessageUpwards("AddLocation", report);
        }
    }
    ```

3. Define the OnTriggerExit function for the inverse procedure

    ```
    public void OnTriggerExit(Collider col)
    {
        string objName = col.gameObject.name;
        if (objName.Equals("Agent") || objName.Equals("Player"))
        {
    ```

```
        VertexReport report = new VertexReport(id, col.
gameObject);
        SendMessageUpwards("RemoveLocation", report);
    }
}
```

4. Create the `GraphDirichlet` class deriving from `Graph`:

```
using UnityEngine;
using System.Collections.Generic;

public class GraphDirichlet : Graph
{
    Dictionary<int, List<int>> objToVertex;
}
```

5. Implement the `AddLocation` function we called before:

```
public void AddLocation(VertexReport report)
{
    int objId = report.obj.GetInstanceID();
    if (!objToVertex.ContainsKey(objId))
    {
        objToVertex.Add(objId, new List<int>());
    }
    objToVertex[objId].Add(report.vertex);
}
```

6. Define the `RemoveLocation` function as well:

```
public void RemoveLocation(VertexReport report)
{
    int objId = report.obj.GetInstanceID();
    objToVertex[objId].Remove(report.vertex);
}
```

7. Override the `Start` function to initialize the member variables:

```
public override void Start()
{
    base.Start();
    objToVertex = new Dictionary<int, List<int>>();
}
```

8. Implement the `Load` function for connecting everything:

```
public override void Load()
{
    Vertex[] verts = GameObject.FindObjectsOfType<Vertex>();
    vertices = new List<Vertex>(verts);
```

```
    for (int i = 0; i < vertices.Count; i++)
    {
        VertexVisibility vv = vertices[i] as VertexVisibility;
        vv.id = i;
        vv.FindNeighbours(vertices);
    }
}
```

9. Override the `GetNearestVertex` function:

```
public override Vertex GetNearestVertex(Vector3 position)
{
    Vertex vertex = null;
    float dist = Mathf.Infinity;
    float distNear = dist;
    Vector3 posVertex = Vector3.zero;
    for (int i = 0; i < vertices.Count; i++)
    {
        posVertex = vertices[i].transform.position;
        dist = Vector3.Distance(position, posVertex);
        if (dist < distNear)
        {
            distNear = dist;
            vertex = vertices[i];
        }
    }
    return vertex;
}
```

10. Define the `GetNearestVertex` function, this time with a GameObject as input:

```
public Vertex GetNearestVertex(GameObject obj)
{
    int objId = obj.GetInstanceID();
    Vector3 objPos = obj.transform.position;
    if (!objToVertex.ContainsKey(objId))
        return null;
    List<int> vertIds = objToVertex[objId];
    Vertex vertex = null;
    float dist = Mathf.Infinity;
    for (int i = 0; i < vertIds.Count; i++)
    {
        int id = vertIds[i];
        Vertex v = vertices[id];
        Vector3 vPos = v.transform.position;
        float d = Vector3.Distance(objPos, vPos);
```

```
            if (d < dist)
            {
                vertex = v;
                dist = d;
            }
        }
        return vertex;
    }
```

11. Implement the `GetNeighbors` function:

```
public override Vertex[] GetNeighbours(Vertex v)
{
    List<Edge> edges = v.neighbours;
    Vertex[] ns = new Vertex[edges.Count];
    int i;
    for (i = 0; i < edges.Count; i++)
    {
        ns[i] = edges[i].vertex;
    }
    return ns;
}
```

12. Finally, define the `GetEdges` function:

```
public override Edge[] GetEdges(Vertex v)
{
    return vertices[v.id].neighbours.ToArray();
}
```

How it works...

When the agents or players enter into the area of a vertex, it sends a message to the graph parent class, and indexes that vertex into the proper dictionary of objects, making the appropriate quantization easier. The same inverse principle applies when the player leaves the area. When the player is mapped into more than one vertex, the function returns the index of the closest one.

Also, we're using a dictionary to facilitate the process of translating object instance IDs to the indices of our vertex array.

There's more...

Take into account that placing the vertices and making the connections between them (edges) must be done manually using the implemented method. You're encouraged to implement a way for getting a vertex's neighbors aimed at your own project if you need a more user-friendly (or automated) technique.

Finally, we'll explore is an automated way to get a vertex's neighbors in the next recipe, using ray casting that will probably serve as a starting point.

See also

▶ The *Representing the world with points of visibility* recipe

Representing the world with points of visibility

This is another widely-used technique for world representation based on points located throughout the valid area of navigation, whether manually placed or automated via scripting. We'll be using manually-placed points connected automatically via scripting.

Getting ready

Just like the previous representation, it's important to have several things in order before continuing:

▶ Having the Edge class prepended to the Graph class in the same file

▶ Defining the GetEdges function in the Graph class

▶ Having the Vertex class

The vertex objects in the scene must have a collider component attached to them, as well as the Vertex tag assigned. It's recommended for them to be unitary Sphere primitives.

How to do it...

We'll be creating the graph representation class as well as a custom `Vertex` class:

1. Create the `VertexVisibility` class deriving from `Vertex`:

```
using UnityEngine;
using System.Collections.Generic;

public class VertexVisibility : Vertex
{
    void Awake()
    {
        neighbours = new List<Edge>();
    }
}
```

2. Define the `FindNeighbours` function for automating the process of connecting vertices among them:

```
public void FindNeighbours(List<Vertex> vertices)
{
    Collider c = gameObject.GetComponent<Collider>();
    c.enabled = false;
    Vector3 direction = Vector3.zero;
    Vector3 origin = transform.position;
    Vector3 target = Vector3.zero;
    RaycastHit[] hits;
    Ray ray;
    float distance = 0f;
    // next step
}
```

3. Go over each object and cast a ray to validate whether it's completely visible and then add it to the list of neighbors:

```
for (int i = 0; i < vertices.Count; i++)
{
    if (vertices[i] == this)
        continue;
    target = vertices[i].transform.position;
    direction = target - origin;
    distance = direction.magnitude;
    ray = new Ray(origin, direction);
    hits = Physics.RaycastAll(ray, distance);
    if (hits.Length == 1)
    {
```

```
            if (hits[0].collider.gameObject.tag.Equals("Vertex"))
            {
                Edge e = new Edge();
                e.cost = distance;
                GameObject go = hits[0].collider.gameObject;
                Vertex v = go.GetComponent<Vertex>();
                if (v != vertices[i])
                    continue;
                e.vertex = v;
                neighbours.Add(e);
            }
        }
    }
    c.enabled = true;
```

4. Create the `GraphVisibility` class:

```
using UnityEngine;
using System.Collections.Generic;

public class GraphVisibility : Graph
{
    // next steps
}
```

5. Build the `Load` function for making the connections between vertices:

```
public override void Load()
{
    Vertex[] verts = GameObject.FindObjectsOfType<Vertex>();
    vertices = new List<Vertex>(verts);
    for (int i = 0; i < vertices.Count; i++)
    {
        VertexVisibility vv = vertices[i] as VertexVisibility;
        vv.id = i;
        vv.FindNeighbours(vertices);
    }
}
```

6. Define the `GetNearesteVertex` function:

```
public override Vertex GetNearestVertex(Vector3 position)
{
    Vertex vertex = null;
    float dist = Mathf.Infinity;
    float distNear = dist;
    Vector3 posVertex = Vector3.zero;
```

```
        for (int i = 0; i < vertices.Count; i++)
        {
            posVertex = vertices[i].transform.position;
            dist = Vector3.Distance(position, posVertex);
            if (dist < distNear)
            {
                distNear = dist;
                vertex = vertices[i];
            }
        }
        return vertex;
    }
```

7. Define the `GetNeighbours` function:

```
public override Vertex[] GetNeighbours(Vertex v)
{
    List<Edge> edges = v.neighbours;
    Vertex[] ns = new Vertex[edges.Count];
    int i;
    for (i = 0; i < edges.Count; i++)
    {
        ns[i] = edges[i].vertex;
    }
    return ns;
}
```

8. Finally, override the `GetEdges` function:

```
public override Edge[] GetEdges(Vertex v)
{
    return vertices[v.id].neighbours.ToArray();
}
```

How it works...

The parent class `GraphVisibility` indexes every vertex on the scene and makes use of the `FindNeighbours` function on each one. This is in order to build the graph and make the connections without total user supervision, beyond placing the visibility points where the user sees fit. Also, the distance between two points is used to assign the cost to that corresponding edge.

There's more...

It's important to make a point visible to one another for the graph to be connected. This approach is also suitable for building intelligent graphs considering stairs and cliffs, it just requires moving the `Load` function to an editor-friendly class in order to call it in edit mode, and then modify or delete the corresponding edges to make it work as intended.

Take a look at the previous recipe's *Getting ready* section so you can better understand the starting point in case you feel you're missing something.

For further information about custom editors, editor scripting, and how to execute code in edit mode, please refer to the Unity documentation, available online at:

- ▶ `http://docs.unity3d.com/ScriptReference/Editor.html`
- ▶ `http://docs.unity3d.com/ScriptReference/ExecuteInEditMode.html`
- ▶ `http://docs.unity3d.com/Manual/PlatformDependentCompilation.html`

See also

- ▶ *Representing the world with Dirichlet domains* recipe

Representing the world with a self-made navigation mesh

Sometimes, a custom navigation mesh is necessary for dealing with difficult situations such as different types of graphs, but placing the graph's vertices manually is troublesome because it requires a lot of time to cover large areas.

We will learn how to use a model's mesh in order to generate a navigation mesh based on its triangles' centroids as vertices, and then leverage the heavy lifting from the previous recipe we learned.

Getting ready

This recipe requires some knowledge of custom editor scripting and understanding and implementing the points of visibility in the graph representation. Also, it is worth mentioning that the script instantiates a `CustomNavMesh` game object automatically in the scene and requires a prefab assigned, just like any other graph representation.

Finally, it's important to create the following class, deriving from `GraphVisibility`:

```
using UnityEngine;
using System.Collections;
using System.Collections.Generic;

public class CustomNavMesh : GraphVisibility
{
    public override void Start()
    {
        instIdToId = new Dictionary<int, int>();
    }
}
```

How to do it...

We will create an editor window for easily handling the automation process without weighing down the graph's `Start` function, delaying the scene loading.

1. Create the `CustomNavMeshWindow` class and place it in a directory called `Editor`:

```
using UnityEngine;
using UnityEditor;
using System.Collections;
using System.Collections.Generic;

public class CustomNavMeshWindow : EditorWindow
{
    // next steps here
}
```

2. Add the attributes to the editor window:

```
static bool isEnabled = false;
static GameObject graphObj;
static CustomNavMesh graph;
static CustomNavMeshWindow window;
static GameObject graphVertex;
```

3. Implement the function for initializing and showing the window:

```
[MenuItem("UAIPC/Ch02/CustomNavMeshWindow")]
static void Init()
{
    window = EditorWindow.GetWindow<CustomNavMeshWindow>();
    window.title = "CustomNavMeshWindow";
    SceneView.onSceneGUIDelegate += OnScene;
```

```
        graphObj = GameObject.Find("CustomNavMesh");
        if (graphObj == null)
        {
            graphObj = new GameObject("CustomNavMesh");
            graphObj.AddComponent<CustomNavMesh>();
            graph = graphObj.GetComponent<CustomNavMesh>();
        }
        else
        {
            graph = graphObj.GetComponent<CustomNavMesh>();
            if (graph == null)
                graphObj.AddComponent<CustomNavMesh>();
            graph = graphObj.GetComponent<CustomNavMesh>();
        }
    }
```

4. Define the OnDestroy function:

```
void OnDestroy()
{
    SceneView.onSceneGUIDelegate -= OnScene;
}
```

5. Implement the OnGUI function for drawing the window's interior:

```
void OnGUI()
{
    isEnabled = EditorGUILayout.Toggle("Enable Mesh Picking",
isEnabled);
    if (GUILayout.Button("Build Edges"))
    {
        if (graph != null)
            graph.LoadGraph();
    }
}
```

6. Implement the first half of the OnScene function for handling the left-click on the scene window:

```
private static void OnScene(SceneView sceneView)
{
    if (!isEnabled)
        return;
    if (Event.current.type == EventType.MouseDown)
    {
        graphVertex = graph.vertexPrefab;
        if (graphVertex == null)
```

```
        {
            Debug.LogError("No Vertex Prefab assigned");
            return;
        }
        Event e = Event.current;
        Ray ray = HandleUtility.GUIPointToWorldRay(e.
mousePosition);
        RaycastHit hit;
        GameObject newV;
        // next step
    }
}
```

7. Implement the second half for implementing the behavior when clicking on the mesh:

```
if (Physics.Raycast(ray, out hit))
{
    GameObject obj = hit.collider.gameObject;
    Mesh mesh = obj.GetComponent<MeshFilter>().sharedMesh;
    Vector3 pos;
    int i;
    for (i = 0; i < mesh.triangles.Length; i += 3)
    {
        int i0 = mesh.triangles[i];
        int i1 = mesh.triangles[i + 1];
        int i2 = mesh.triangles[i + 2];
        pos = mesh.vertices[i0];
        pos += mesh.vertices[i1];
        pos += mesh.vertices[i2];
        pos /= 3;
        newV = (GameObject)Instantiate(graphVertex, pos,
Quaternion.identity);
        newV.transform.Translate(obj.transform.position);
        newV.transform.parent = graphObj.transform;
        graphObj.transform.parent = obj.transform;
    }
}
```

How it works...

We create a custom editor window and set up the delegate function OnScene for handling events on the scene window. Also, we create the graph nodes by traversing the mesh vertex arrays, computing each triangle's centroid. Finally, we make use of the graph's LoadGraph function in order to compute neighbors.

Finding your way out of a maze with DFS

The **Depth-First Search (DFS)** algorithm is a path-finding technique suitable for low-memory devices. Another common use is to build mazes with a few modifications to the list of nodes visited and discovered, however the main algorithm stays the same.

Getting ready

This is a high-level algorithm that relies on each graph's implementation of the general functions, so the algorithm is implemented in the Graph class.

It is important to

How to do it...

Even though this recipe is only defining a function, please take into consideration the comments in the code to understand the indentation and code flow for effectively:

1. Declare the GetPathDFS function:

```
public List<Vertex> GetPathDFS(GameObject srcObj, GameObject dstObj)
{
    // next steps
}
```

2. Validate if input objects are null:

```
if (srcObj == null || dstObj == null)
    return new List<Vertex>();
```

3. Declare and initialize the variables we need for the algorithm:

```
Vertex src = GetNearestVertex(srcObj.transform.position);
Vertex dst = GetNearestVertex(dstObj.transform.position);
Vertex[] neighbours;
Vertex v;
int[] previous = new int[vertices.Count];
for (int i = 0; i < previous.Length; i++)
    previous[i] = -1;
previous[src.id] = src.id;
Stack<Vertex> s = new Stack<Vertex>();
s.Push(src);
```

4. Implement the DFS algorithm for finding a path:

```
while (s.Count != 0)
{
    v = s.Pop();
    if (ReferenceEquals(v, dst))
    {
        return BuildPath(src.id, v.id, ref previous);
    }

    neighbours = GetNeighbours(v);
    foreach (Vertex n in neighbours)
    {
        if (previous[n.id] != -1)
            continue;
        previous[n.id] = v.id;
        s.Push(n);
    }
}
```

How it works...

The algorithm is based on the iterative version of DFS. It is also based on the in-order traversing of a graph and the LIFO philosophy using a stack for visiting nodes and adding discovered ones.

There is more...

We called the function `BuildPath`, but we haven't implemented it yet. It is important to note that this function is called by almost every other path-finding algorithm in this chapter, that's why it's not part of the main recipe.

This is the code for the `BuildPath` method:

```
private List<Vertex> BuildPath(int srcId, int dstId, ref int[] prevList)
{
    List<Vertex> path = new List<Vertex>();
    int prev = dstId;
    do
    {
        path.Add(vertices[prev]);
        prev = prevList[prev];
    } while (prev != srcId);
    return path;
}
```

Finding the shortest path in a grid with BFS

The **Breadth-First Search (BFS)** algorithm is another basic technique for graph traversal and it's aimed to get the shortest path in the fewest steps possible, with the trade-off being expensive in terms of memory; thus, aimed specially at games on high-end consoles and computers.

Getting ready

This is a high-level algorithm that relies on each graph's implementation of the general functions, so the algorithm is implemented in the `Graph` class.

How to do it...

Even though this recipe is only defining a function, please take into consideration the comments in the code to understand the indentation and code flow more effectively:

1. Declare the `GetPathBFS` function:

```
public List<Vertex> GetPathBFS(GameObject srcObj, GameObject
dstObj)
{
    if (srcObj == null || dstObj == null)
        return new List<Vertex>();
    // next steps
}
```

2. Declare and initialize the variables we need for the algorithm:

```
Vertex[] neighbours;
Queue<Vertex> q = new Queue<Vertex>();
Vertex src = GetNearestVertex(srcObj.transform.position);
Vertex dst = GetNearestVertex(dstObj.transform.position);
Vertex v;
int[] previous = new int[vertices.Count];
for (int i = 0; i < previous.Length; i++)
    previous[i] = -1;
previous[src.id] = src.id;
q.Enqueue(src);
```

3. Implement the BFS algorithm for finding a path:

```
while (q.Count != 0)
{
    v = q.Dequeue();
    if (ReferenceEquals(v, dst))
```

```
        {
            return BuildPath(src.id, v.id, ref previous);
        }

        neighbours = GetNeighbours(v);
        foreach (Vertex n in neighbours)
        {
            if (previous[n.id] != -1)
                continue;
            previous[n.id] = v.id;
            q.Enqueue(n);
        }
    }
    return new List<Vertex>();
```

How it works...

The BFS algorithm is similar to the DFS algorithm because it's based on the same in-order traversing of a graph but, instead of a stack such as DFS, BFS uses a queue for visiting the discovered nodes.

There is more...

In case you haven't noticed, we didn't implement the method `BuildPath`. This is because we talked about it at the end of the Depth-First Search recipe.

See also

▸ *Finding your way out of a maze with DFS*, recipe.

Finding the shortest path with Dijkstra

The Dijkstra's algorithm was initially designed to solve the single-source shortest path problem for a graph. Thus, the algorithm finds the lowest-cost route to everywhere from a single point. We will learn how to make use of it with two different approaches.

Getting ready

The first thing to do is import the binary heap class from the **Game Programming Wiki (GPWiki)** into our project, given that neither the .Net framework nor Mono has a defined structure for handling binary heaps or priority queues.

For downloading the source file and more information regarding GP Wiki's binary heap, please refer to the documentation online available at `http://content.gpwiki.org/index.php/C_sharp:BinaryHeapOfT`.

How to do it...

We will learn how to implement the Dijkstra algorithm using the same number of parameters as the other algorithms, and then explain how to modify it to make maximum use of it according to its original purpose.

1. Define the `GetPathDijkstra` function with its internal variables:

```
public List<Vertex> GetPathDijkstra(GameObject srcObj, GameObject
dstObj)
{
    if (srcObj == null || dstObj == null)
        return new List<Vertex>();
    Vertex src = GetNearestVertex(srcObj.transform.position);
    Vertex dst = GetNearestVertex(dstObj.transform.position);
    GPWiki.BinaryHeap<Edge> frontier = new GPWiki.
BinaryHeap<Edge>();
    Edge[] edges;
    Edge node, child;
    int size = vertices.Count;
    float[] distValue = new float[size];
    int[] previous = new int[size];

    // next steps
}
```

2. Add the source node to the heap (working as a priority queue) and assign a distance value of infinity to all of them but the source node:

```
node = new Edge(src, 0);
frontier.Add(node);
distValue[src.id] = 0;
previous[src.id] = src.id;
for (int i = 0; i < size; i++)
{
    if (i == src.id)
        continue;
    distValue[i] = Mathf.Infinity;
    previous[i] = -1;
}
```

3. Define a loop to iterate while the queue is not empty:

```
while (frontier.Count != 0)
{
    node = frontier.Remove();
    int nodeId = node.vertex.id;
    // next steps
}
return new List<Vertex>();
```

4. Code the procedure when arriving at the destination:

```
if (ReferenceEquals(node.vertex, dst))
{
    return BuildPath(src.id, node.vertex.id, ref previous);
}
```

5. Otherwise, process the visited nodes and add its neighbors to the queue, and return the path (not empty if there is a path from source to destination vertex):

```
edges = GetEdges(node.vertex);
foreach (Edge e in edges)
{
    int eId = e.vertex.id;
    if (previous[eId] != -1)
        continue;
    float cost = distValue[nodeId] + e.cost;
    if (cost < distValue[e.vertex.id])
    {
        distValue[eId] = cost;
        previous[eId] = nodeId;
        frontier.Remove(e);
        child = new Edge(e.vertex, cost);
        frontier.Add(child);
    }
}
```

How it works...

The Dijkstra algorithm works in a similar way to BFS, but considers non-negative edge costs in order to build the best route from the source vertex to every other one. That's why we have an array for storing the previous vertex.

There's more...

We will learn how to modify the current Dijkstra algorithm in order to approach the problem using pre-processing techniques and optimizing the path-finding time. It can be seen as three big steps: modifying the main algorithm, creating the pre-processing function (handy in editor mode, for example), and, finally, defining the path-retrieval function.

1. Modify the main function's signature:

    ```
    public int[] Dijkstra(GameObject srcObj)
    ```

2. Change the returning value:

    ```
    return previous;
    ```

3. Remove the lines from step 4 in the *How to do it* section:

4. Also, delete the following line at the beginning:

    ```
    Vertex dst = GetNearestVertex(dstObj.transform.position);
    ```

5. Create a new member value to the `Graph` class:

    ```
    List<int[]> routes = new List<int[]>();
    ```

6. Define the pre-processing function, called `DijkstraProcessing`:

    ```
    public void DijkstraProcessing()
    {
        int size = GetSize();
        for (int i = 0; i < size; i++)
        {
            GameObject go = vertices[i].gameObject;
            routes.add(Dijkstra(go));
        }
    }
    ```

7. Implement a new `GetPathDijkstra` function for path retrieval:

    ```
    public List<Vertex> GetPathDijkstra(GameObject srcObj, GameObject dstObj)
    {
        List<Vertex> path = new List<Vertex>();
        Vertex src = GetNearestVertex(srcObj);
        Vertex dst = GetNearestVertex(dstObj);
        return BuildPath(src.id, dst.id, ref routes[dst.id]);
    }
    ```

In case you haven't noticed, we didn't implement the method `BuildPath`. This is because we talked about it at the end of the Depth-First Search recipe.

▸ *Finding your way out of a maze with DFS*, recipe.

Finding the best-promising path with A*

The A* algorithm is probably the most-used technique for path finding, given its implementation simplicity, and efficiency, and because it has room for optimization. It's no coincidence that there are several algorithms based on it. At the same time, A* shares some roots with the Dijkstra algorithm, so you'll find similarities in their implementations.

Getting ready

Just like Dijkstra's algorithm, this recipe uses the binary heap extracted from the GPWiki. Also, it is important to understand what delegates are and how they work for. Finally, we are entering into the world of informed search; that means that we need to understand what a heuristic is and what it is for.

In a nutshell, for the purpose of this recipe, a heuristic is a function for calculating the approximate cost between two vertices in order to compare them to other alternatives and take the minimum-cost choice.

We need to add small changes to the Graph class:

1. Define a member variable as delegate:

   ```
   public delegate float Heuristic(Vertex a, Vertex b);
   ```

2. Implement Euclidean distance member function to use it as default heuristic:

   ```
   public float EuclidDist(Vertex a, Vertex b)
   {
       Vector3 posA = a.transform.position;
       Vector3 posB = b.transform.position;
       return  Vector3.Distance(posA, posB);
   }
   ```

3. Implement Manhattan distance function to use as a different heuristic. It will help us in comparing results using different heuristics:

   ```
   public float ManhattanDist(Vertex a, Vertex b)
   {
       Vector3 posA = a.transform.position;
       Vector3 posB = b.transform.position;
       return Mathf.Abs(posA.x - posB.x) + Mathf.Abs(posA.y -
   posB.y);
   }
   ```

How to do it...

Even though this recipe covers defining a function, please take into consideration the comments in the code to understand the indentation and code flow more effectively:

1. Define the `GetPathAstar` function along with its member variables:

```
public List<Vertex> GetPathAstar(GameObject srcObj, GameObject
dstObj, Heuristic h = null)
{
    if (srcObj == null || dstObj == null)
        return new List<Vertex>();
    if (ReferenceEquals(h, null))
        h = EuclidDist;

    Vertex src = GetNearestVertex(srcObj.transform.position);
    Vertex dst = GetNearestVertex(dstObj.transform.position);
    GPWiki.BinaryHeap<Edge> frontier = new GPWiki.
BinaryHeap<Edge>();
    Edge[] edges;
    Edge node, child;
    int size = vertices.Count;
    float[] distValue = new float[size];
    int[] previous = new int[size];
    // next steps
}
```

2. Add the source node to the heap (working as a priority queue) and assign a distance value of infinity to all of them but the source node:

```
node = new Edge(src, 0);
frontier.Add(node);
distValue[src.id] = 0;
previous[src.id] = src.id;
for (int i = 0; i < size; i++)
{
    if (i == src.id)
        continue;
    distValue[i] = Mathf.Infinity;
    previous[i] = -1;
}
```

3. Declare the loop for traversing the graph:

```
while (frontier.Count != 0)
{
    // next steps
}
return new List<Vertex>();
```

4. Implement the conditions for returning a path when necessary:

```
node = frontier.Remove();
int nodeId = node.vertex.id;
if (ReferenceEquals(node.vertex, dst))
{
    return BuildPath(src.id, node.vertex.id, ref previous);
}
```

5. Get the vertex's neighbors (also called `successors` in some text books):

```
edges = GetEdges(node.vertex);
```

6. Traverse the neighbors for computing the `cost` function:

```
foreach (Edge e in edges)
{
    int eId = e.vertex.id;
    if (previous[eId] != -1)
        continue;
    float cost = distValue[nodeId] + e.cost;
    // key point
    cost += h(node.vertex, e.vertex);
    // next step
}
```

7. Expand the list of explored nodes (frontier) and updating costs, if necessary:

```
if (cost < distValue[e.vertex.id])
{
    distValue[eId] = cost;
    previous[eId] = nodeId;
    frontier.Remove(e);
    child = new Edge(e.vertex, cost);
    frontier.Add(child);
}
```

How it works...

A* works in a similar fashion to Dijkstra's algorithm. However, instead of choosing the real lowest-cost node from all the possible options, it chooses the most-promising one based on a given heuristic, and goes on from there. In our case, the default heuristic is based solely on the Euclidian distance between two vertices with the option of using Manhattan distance.

There's more...

You are welcome to play with different heuristic functions depending on the game and context, and the following is an example of how to do so:

1. Define a heuristic function in the `Graph` class:

```
public float Heuristic(Vertex a, Vertex b)
{
    float estimation = 0f;
    // your logic here
    return estimation;
}
```

The important thing here is that the heuristic we develop is both *admissible* and *consistent*. For more theoretical insights about these topics, please refer to *Artificial Intelligence: A Modern Approach* by Russel and Norvig.

In case you haven't noticed, we didn't implement the method `BuildPath`. This is because we talked about it at the end of the Depth-First Search recipe.

See also

 ▸ The *Finding the shortest path with Dijkstra* recipe

 ▸ The *Finding your way out of a maze with DFS* recipe

For further information about Delegates, please refer to the official documentation available online at:

 ▸ `https://unity3d.com/learn/tutorials/modules/intermediate/scripting/delegates`

Improving A* for memory: IDA*

IDA* is a variant of an algorithm called Iterative Deepening Depth-First Search. Its memory usage is lower than A* because it doesn't make use of data structures to store the looked-up and explored nodes.

Getting ready

For this recipe, it is important to have some understanding of how recursion works.

How to do it...

This is a long recipe that can be seen as an extensive two-step process: creating the main function, and creating an internal recursive one. Please take into consideration the comments in the code to understand the indentation and code flow more effectively:

1. Let's start by defining the main function called `GetPathIDAstar`:

```
public List<Vertex> GetPathIDAstar(GameObject srcObj, GameObject
dstObj, Heuristic h = null)
{
    if (srcObj == null || dstObj == null)
        return new List<Vertex>();
    if (ReferenceEquals(h, null))
        h = EuclidDist;
    // next steps;
}
```

2. Declare and compute the variables to use along with the algorithm:

```
List<Vertex> path = new List<Vertex>();
Vertex src = GetNearestVertex(srcObj.transform.position);
Vertex dst = GetNearestVertex(dstObj.transform.position);
Vertex goal = null;
bool[] visited = new bool[vertices.Count];
for (int i = 0; i < visited.Length; i++)
visited[i] = false;
visited[src.id] = true;
```

3. Implement the algorithm's loop:

```
float bound = h(src, dst);
while (bound < Mathf.Infinity)
{
    bound = RecursiveIDAstar(src, dst, bound, h, ref goal, ref
visited);
}
if (ReferenceEquals(goal, null))
    return path;
return BuildPath(goal);
```

4. Now it's time to build the recursive internal function:

```
private float RecursiveIDAstar(
        Vertex v,
        Vertex dst,
        float bound,
        Heuristic h,
        ref Vertex goal,
        ref bool[] visited)
{
    // next steps
}
```

5. Prepare everything to start the recursion:

```
// base case
if (ReferenceEquals(v, dst))
    return Mathf.Infinity;
Edge[] edges = GetEdges(v);
if (edges.Length == 0)
    return Mathf.Infinity;
```

6. Apply the recursion for each neighbor:

```
// recursive case
float fn = Mathf.Infinity;
foreach (Edge e in edges)
{
    int eId = e.vertex.id;
    if (visited[eId])
        continue;
    visited[eId] = true;
    e.vertex.prev = v;
    float f = h(v, dst);
    float b;
    if (f <= bound)
    {
        b = RecursiveIDAstar(e.vertex, dst, bound, h, ref goal,
ref visited);
        fn = Mathf.Min(f, b);
    }
    else
        fn = Mathf.Min(fn, f);
}
```

7. Return a value based on the recursion result:

```
return fn;
```

How it works...

As we can see, the algorithm is very similar to that of the recursive version of Depth-First Search, but uses the principle of making decisions on top of a heuristic from A*. The main function is responsible for starting the recursion and building the resulting path. The recursive function is the one responsible for traversing the graph, looking for the destination node.

There is more...

This time we will need to implement a different a `BuildPath` function, in case you have followed along with the previous path finding recipes. Otherwise, we will need to implement this method that we haven't defined yet:

```
private List<Vertex> BuildPath(Vertex v)
{
    List<Vertex> path = new List<Vertex>();
    while (!ReferenceEquals(v, null))
    {
        path.Add(v);
        v = v.prev;
    }
    return path;
}
```

Planning navigation in several frames: time-sliced search

When dealing with large graphs, computing paths can take a lot of time, even halting the game for a couple of seconds. This could ruins its overall experience, to say the least. Luckily enough there are methods to avoid this.

 This recipe is built on top of the principle of using coroutines as a method to keep the game running smoothly while finding a path in the background; some knowledge about coroutines is required.

Getting ready

We'll learn how to implement path-finding techniques using coroutines by refactoring the A* algorithm learned previously, but we will handle its signature as a different function.

How to do it...

Even though this recipe is only defining a function, please take into consideration the comments in the code to understand the indentation and code flow more effectively:

1. Modify the `Graph` class and add a couple of member variables. One for storing the path and the other to know whether the coroutine has finished:

```
public List<Vertex> path;
public bool isFinished;
```

2. Declare the member function:

```
public IEnumerator GetPathInFrames(GameObject srcObj, GameObject
dstObj, Heuristic h = null)
{
    //next steps
}
```

3. Include the following member variables at the beginning:

```
isFinished = false;
path = new List<Vertex>();
if (srcObj == null || dstObj == null)
{
    path = new List<Vertex>();
    isFinished = true;
    yield break;
}
```

4. Modify the loop to traverse the graph:

```
while (frontier.Count != 0)
{
    // changes over A*
    yield return null;
    ////////////////////////////
    node = frontier.Remove();
```

5. Also, include the other path-retrieval validations:

```
if (ReferenceEquals(node.vertex, dst))
{
    // changes over A*
    path = BuildPath(src.id, node.vertex.id, ref previous);
    break;
    ////////////////////////////
}
```

6. Finally, reset the proper values and return control at the end of the function, after closing the main loop:

```
isFinished = true;
yield break;
```

How it works...

The yield return null statement inside the main loop works as a flag for delivering control to the higher-level functions, thus computing each new loop in each new frame using Unity's internal multi-tasking system.

See also

▸ The *Finding the best-promising path with A** recipe

For further information about Coroutines and more examples, please refer to the official documentation available online at:

▸ `http://docs.unity3d.com/Manual/Coroutines.html`

▸ `https://unity3d.com/learn/tutorials/modules/intermediate/scripting/coroutines`

Smoothing a path

When dealing with regular-size vertices on graph, such as grids, it's pretty common to see some kind of *robotic* movement from the agents in the game. Depending on the type of game we're developing, this could be avoided using path-smoothing techniques, such as the one we're about to learn.

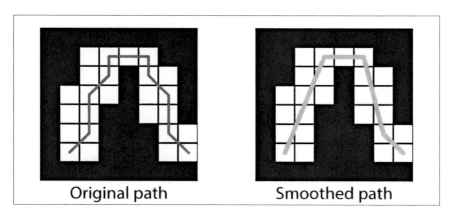

Original path   Smoothed path

Getting ready

Let's define a new tag in the Unity editor called `Wall` and assign it to every object in the scene that is intended to work as a wall or obstacle in the navigation.

How to do it...

This is an easy, yet powerful, function:

1. Define the `Smooth` function:

```
public List<Vertex> Smooth(List<Vertex> path)
{
    // next steps here
}
```

2. Check whether it is worth computing a new path:

```
List<Vertex> newPath = new List<Vertex>();
if (path.Count == 0)
    return newPath;
if (path.Count < 3)
    return path;
```

3. Implement the loops for traversing the list and building the new path:

```
newPath.Add(path[0]);
int i, j;
for (i = 0; i < path.Count - 1;)
{
    for (j = i + 1; j < path.Count; j++)
    {
        // next steps here
    }
    i = j - 1;
    newPath.Add(path[i]);
}
return newPath;
```

4. Declare and compute the variables to be used by the ray casting function:

```
Vector3 origin = path[i].transform.position;
Vector3 destination = path[j].transform.position;
Vector3 direction = destination - origin;
float distance = direction.magnitude;
bool isWall = false;
direction.Normalize();
```

5. Cast a ray from the current starting node to the next one:

```
Ray ray = new Ray(origin, direction);
RaycastHit[] hits;
hits = Physics.RaycastAll(ray, distance);
```

6. Check whether there is a wall and break the loop accordingly:

```
foreach (RaycastHit hit in hits)
{
    string tag = hit.collider.gameObject.tag;
    if (tag.Equals("Wall"))
    {
        isWall = true;
        break;
    }
}
if (isWall)
    break;
```

How it works...

We create a new path, taking the initial node as a starting point, and apply ray casting to the following node in the path, until we get a collision with a wall. When that happens, we take the previous node as the following node in the new path and the starting point for traversing the original one, until there are no nodes left to check. That way, we build a more intuitive path.

3
Decision Making

In this chapter, we will cover the following recipes:

- ▶ Choosing through a decision tree
- ▶ Working a finite-state machine
- ▶ Improving FSMs: hierarchical finite-state machines
- ▶ Combining FSMs and decision trees
- ▶ Implementing behavior trees
- ▶ Working with fuzzy logic
- ▶ Representing states with numerical values: Markov system
- ▶ Making decisions with goal-oriented behaviors

Introduction

Making decisions or changing the game flow according to the game's state could get really messy if we rely only on simple control structures. That's why we will learn different decision-making techniques that are flexible enough to adapt to different types of games, and robust enough to let us build modular decision-making systems.

The techniques covered in the chapter are mostly related to trees, automata, and matrices. Also, some topics require a good understanding of how recursion, inheritance, and polymorphism work, so it is important that we review those topics if that is the case.

Choosing through a decision tree

One of the simplest mechanisms for tackling decision-making problems is decision trees, because they are fast and easy to grasp and implement. As a consequence, it's one of the most used techniques today; it is extensively used in other character-controlled scopes such as animations.

Getting ready

This recipe requires a good understanding of recursion and inheritance as we will constantly be implementing and calling virtual functions throughout the sections.

How to do it...

This recipe requires a lot of attention due to the number of files that we will need to handle. Overall, we will create a parent class `DecisionTreeNode`, from which we will derive the other ones. Finally, we will learn how to implement a couple of standard decision nodes:

1. First, create the parent class, `DecisionTreeNode`:

```
using UnityEngine;
using System.Collections;
public class DecisionTreeNode : MonoBehaviour
{
    public virtual DecisionTreeNode MakeDecision()
    {
        return null;
    }
}
```

2. Create the pseudo-abstract class, `Decision`, deriving from the parent class, `DecisionTreeNode`:

```
using UnityEngine;
using System.Collections;
public class Decision : DecisionTreeNode
{
    public Action nodeTrue;
    public Action nodeFalse;

    public virtual Action GetBranch()
    {
        return null;
    }
}
```

3. Define the pseudo-abstract class, `Action`:

```
using UnityEngine;
using System.Collections;
public class Action : DecisionTreeNode
{
    public bool activated = false;

    public override DecisionTreeNode MakeDecision()
    {
        return this;
    }
}
```

4. Implement the virtual function, `LateUpdate`:

```
public virtual void LateUpdate()
{
    if (!activated)
        return;
    // Implement your behaviors here
}
```

5. Create the final class, `DecisionTree`:

```
using UnityEngine;
using System.Collections;
public class DecisionTree : DecisionTreeNode
{
    public DecisionTreeNode root;
    private Action actionNew;
    private Action actionOld;
}
```

6. Override the function, `MakeDecision`:

```
public override DecisionTreeNode MakeDecision()
{
    return root.MakeDecision();
}
```

7. Finally, implement the `Update` function:

```
void Update()
{
    actionNew.activated = false;
    actionOld = actionNew;
    actionNew = root.MakeDecision() as Action;
    if (actionNew == null)
```

```
            actionNew = actionOld;
        actionNew.activated = true;
    }
```

How it works...

Decision nodes choose which path to take, calling the `MakeDecision` function recursively. It is worth mentioning that branches must be decisions and leaves must be actions. Also, we should be careful not to create cycles within the tree.

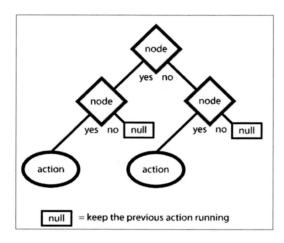

There's more...

We can create custom decisions and actions starting from the pseudo-abstract classes we already created. For example, a decision on whether to attack or run away from the player.

The custom Boolean decision:

```
using UnityEngine;
using System.Collections;

public class DecisionBool : Decision
{
    public bool valueDecision;
    public bool valueTest;

    public override Action GetBranch()
    {
        if (valueTest == valueDecision)
```

```
            return nodeTrue;
        return nodeFalse;
    }
}
```

Working a finite-state machine

Another interesting yet easy-to-implement technique is **finite-state machines (FSM)**. They move us to change the train of thought from what it was in the previous recipe. FSMs are great when our train of thought is more event-oriented, and we think in terms of holding behavior until a condition is met changing to another.

Getting ready

This is a technique mostly based on automata behavior, and will lay the grounds for the next recipe, which is an improved version of the current one.

How to do it...

This recipe breaks down into implementing three classes from the ground up, and everything will make sense by the final step:

1. Implement the Condition class:

    ```
    public class Condition
    {
        public virtual bool Test()
        {
            return false;
        }
    }
    ```

2. Define the Transition class:

    ```
    public class Transition
    {
        public Condition condition;
        public State target;
    }
    ```

3. Define the `State` class:

```
using UnityEngine;
using System.Collections.Generic;

public class State : MonoBehaviour
{
    public List<Transition> transitions;
}
```

4. Implement the Awake function:

```
public virtual void Awake()
{
    transitions = new List<Transition>();
    // TO-DO
    // setup your transitions here
```

5. Define the initialization function:

```
public virtual void OnEnable()
{
    // TO-DO
    // develop state's initialization here
}
```

6. Define the finalization function:

```
public virtual void OnDisable()
{
    // TO-DO
    // develop state's finalization here
}
```

7. Define the function for developing the proper behavior for the state:

```
public virtual void Update()
{
    // TO-DO
    // develop behaviour here
}
```

8. Implement the function for deciding if and which state to enable next:

```
public void LateUpdate()
{
    foreach (Transition t in transitions)
    {
        if (t.condition.Test())
        {
```

```
            t.target.enabled = true;
            this.enabled = false;
            return;
        }
    }
}
```

How it works...

Each state is a `MonoBehaviour` script that is enabled or disabled according to the transitions it comes from; we take advantage of `LateUpdate` in order not to change the usual train of thought when developing behaviors, and we use it to check whether it is time to transition to a different state. It is important to disable every state in the game object apart from the initial one.

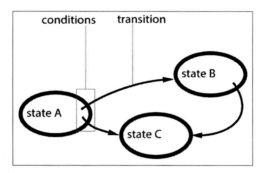

There's more...

In order to illustrate how to develop child classes deriving from `Condition`, let's take a look at a couple of examples: one that is aimed at validating a value in a range and the other one at being a logic comparer between two conditions:

The code for `ConditionFloat` is as follows:

```
using UnityEngine;
using System.Collections;

public class ConditionFloat : Condition
{
    public float valueMin;
    public float valueMax;
    public float valueTest;

    public override bool Test()
```

```
        {
            if (valueMax >= valueTest && valueTest >= valueMin)
                return true;
            return false;
        }
    }
```

The following is an example of code for `ConditionAnd`:

```
using UnityEngine;
using System.Collections;

public class ConditionAnd : Condition
{
    public Condition conditionA;
    public Condition conditionB;

    public override bool Test()
    {
        if (conditionA.Test() && conditionB.Test())
            return true;
        return false;
    }
}
```

Improving FSMs: hierarchical finite-state machines

Finite-state machines can be improved in terms of having different layers or hierarchies. The principles are the same, but states are able to have their own internal finite-state machine, making them more flexible and scalable.

Getting ready

This recipe is based on top of the previous recipe, so it is important that we grasp and understand how the finite-state machine recipe works.

How to do it...

We will create a state that is capable of holding internal states, in order to develop multi-level hierarchical state machines:

1. Create the `StateHighLevel` class deriving from `State`:

    ```
    using UnityEngine;
    using System.Collections;
    using System.Collections.Generic;

    public class StateHighLevel : State
    {
    }
    ```

2. Add the new member variables to control the internal states:

    ```
    public List<State> states;
    public State stateInitial;
    protected State stateCurrent;
    ```

3. Override the initialization function:

    ```
    public override void OnEnable()
    {
        if (stateCurrent == null)
            stateCurrent = stateInitial;
        stateCurrent.enabled = true;
    }
    ```

4. Override the finalization function:

    ```
    public override void OnDisable()
    {
        base.OnDisable();
        stateCurrent.enabled = false;
        foreach (State s in states)
        {
            s.enabled = false;
        }
    }
    ```

How it works...

The high-level state class lets us activate the internal FSMs when it is enabled and recursively disables its internal states when disabled. The working principle stays the same thanks to the list of states and the way the parent class resolves the transitioning process.

Kindly refer to the recipe, *Working a finite-state machine.*

Combining FSMs and decision trees

Given the previous recipes' ease of implementation and learning, we can combine them to develop a powerful decision-making system with benefits from both worlds, making it a very powerful technique in many different scenarios.

Getting ready

We will learn how to make modifications and develop child classes in order to create a finite-state machine that is capable of creating complex transitions based on decision trees.

How to do it...

This recipe relies on creating a couple of child classes from the one we already know and making a little modification:

1. Create a new action class that holds a reference to a state:

    ```
    using UnityEngine;
    using System.Collections;

    public class ActionState : DecisionTreeNode
    {
        public State state;

        public override DecisionTreeNode MakeDecision()
        {
            return this;
        }
    }
    ```

2. Implement a transition class that is able to hold a decision tree:

    ```
    using UnityEngine;
    using System.Collections;

    public class TransitionDecision : Transition
    {
        public DecisionTreeNode root;

        public State GetState()
    ```

```
    {
        ActionState action;
        action = root.MakeDecision() as ActionState;
        return action.state;
    }
}
```

3. Modify the `LateUpdate` function in the `State` class to support both transition types:

```
public void LateUpdate()
{
    foreach (Transition t in transitions)
    {
        if (t.condition.Test())
        {
                State target;
            if (t.GetType().Equals(typeof(TransitionDecision)))

                TransitionDecision td = t as TransitionDecision;
                target = td.GetState();
            }
            else
                target = t.target;
            target.enabled = true;
            this.enabled = false;
            return;
        }
    }
}
```

How it works...

The modification on the `State` class lets us deal with the new type of transition. The new child classes are specific types created to trick both systems and obtain the desired result of having an action node that doesn't do anything itself, but returns a new state to be activated after choosing with a decision tree.

See also

Refer to the following recipes:

- ▶ *Choosing through a decision tree*
- ▶ *Working a finite-state machine*

Implementing behavior trees

Behavior trees can be seen as a synthesis of a number of other artificial intelligence techniques, such as finite-state machines, planning, and decision trees. In fact, they share some resemblance to FSMs, but instead of states, we think in terms of actions spanned across a tree structure.

Getting ready

This recipe requires us to understand Coroutines.

How to do it...

Just like decisions trees, we will create three pseudo-abstract classes for handling the process:

1. Create the base class, `Task`:

```
using UnityEngine;
using System.Collections;
using System.Collections.Generic;

public class Task : MonoBehaviour
{
    public List<Task> children;
    protected bool result = false;
    protected bool isFinished = false;
}
```

2. Implement the finalization function:

```
public virtual void SetResult(bool r)
{
    result = r;
    isFinished = true;
}
```

3. Implement the function for creating behaviors:

```
public virtual IEnumerator Run()
{
    SetResult(true);
    yield break;
}
```

4. Implement the general function for starting behaviors:

```
public virtual IEnumerator RunTask()
{
    yield return StartCoroutine(Run());
}
```

5. Create the ConditionBT class:

```
using UnityEngine;
using System.Collections;

public class ConditionBT : Task
{
    public override IEnumerator Run()
    {
        isFinished = false;
        bool r = false;
        // implement your behaviour here
        // define result (r) whether true or false
        //---------
        SetResult(r);
        yield break;
    }
}
```

6. Create the base class for actions:

```
using UnityEngine;
using System.Collections;

public class ActionBT : Task
{
    public override IEnumerator Run()
    {
        isFinished = false;
        // implement your behaviour here
        //---------
        return base.Run();
    }
}
```

7. Implement the Selector class:

```
using UnityEngine;
using System.Collections;

public class Selector : Task
```

```
    {
        public override void SetResult(bool r)
        {
            if (r == true)
                isFinished = true;
        }

        public override IEnumerator RunTask()
        {
            foreach (Task t in children)
                yield return StartCoroutine(t.RunTask());
        }
    }
```

8. Implement also the Sequence class:

```
using UnityEngine;
using System.Collections;

public class Sequence : Task
{
    public override void SetResult(bool r)
    {
        if (r == true)
            isFinished = true;
    }

    public override IEnumerator RunTask()
    {
        foreach (Task t in children)
            yield return StartCoroutine(t.RunTask());
    }
}
```

How it works...

Behavior trees work in a similar fashion to decision trees. However, the leaf nodes are called tasks and there are some branch nodes that are not conditions, but run a set of tasks in one of two ways; Selector and Sequence. Selectors run a set of tasks and return true when one of their tasks return true, it can be seen as an OR node. Sequences run a set of tasks and return true when all of their tasks return true, it can be seen as an AND node.

See also

For more theoretical insights, refer to Ian Millington's book, *Artificial Intelligence for Games*.

Working with fuzzy logic

There are times when we have to deal with gray areas, instead of binary-based values, to make decisions, and fuzzy logic is a set of mathematical techniques that help us with this task.

Imagine that we're developing an automated driver. A couple of available actions are steering and speed control, both of which have a range of degrees. Deciding how to take a turn, and at which speed, is what will make our driver different and possibly smarter. That's the type of gray area that fuzzy logic helps represent and handle.

Getting ready

This recipe requires a set of states indexed by continuous integer numbers. As this representation varies from game to game, we handle the raw input from such states, along with their *fuzzification*, in order to have a good general-purpose fuzzy decision maker. Finally, the decision maker returns a set of fuzzy values representing the degree of membership of each state.

How to do it...

We will create two base classes and our fuzzy decision maker:

1. Create the parent class, `MembershipFunction`:

```
using UnityEngine;
using System.Collections;

public class MembershipFunction : MonoBehaviour
{
    public int stateId;
    public virtual float GetDOM(object input)
    {
        return 0f;
    }
}
```

2. Implement the `FuzzyRule` class:

```
using System.Collections;
using System.Collections.Generic;

public class FuzzyRule
{
    public List<int> stateIds;
    public int conclusionStateId;
}
```

3. Create the `FuzzyDecisionMaker` class:

```
using UnityEngine;
using System.Collections;
using System.Collections.Generic;

public class FuzzyDecisionMaker : MonoBehaviour
{
}
```

4. Define the decision-making function signature and its member variables:

```
public Dictionary<int,float> MakeDecision(object[] inputs,
MembershipFunction[][] mfList, FuzzyRule[] rules)
{
    Dictionary<int, float> inputDOM = new Dictionary<int,
float>();
    Dictionary<int, float> outputDOM = new Dictionary<int,
float>();
    MembershipFunction memberFunc;
    // next steps
}
```

5. Implement the loops for traversing the inputs and populate the initial degree of membership (DOM) for each state:

```
foreach (object input in inputs)
{
    int r, c;
    for (r = 0; r < mfList.Length; r++)
    {
        for (c = 0; c < mfList[r].Length; c++)
        {
            // next step
        }
    }
}
// steps after next
```

6. Define the body of the innermost loop, which makes use of the proper membership functions to set (or update) the degrees of membership:

```
memberFunc = mfList[r][c];
int mfId = memberFunc.stateId;
float dom = memberFunc.GetDOM(input);
if (!inputDOM.ContainsKey(mfId))
{
    inputDOM.Add(mfId, dom);
    outputDOM.Add(mfId, 0f);
```

```
    }
else
    inputDOM[mfId] = dom;
```

7. Traverse the rules for setting the output degrees of membership:

```
foreach (FuzzyRule rule in rules)
{
    int outputId = rule.conclusionStateId;
    float best = outputDOM[outputId];
    float min = 1f;
    foreach (int state in rule.stateIds)
    {
        float dom = inputDOM[state];
        if (dom < best)
            continue;
        if (dom < min)
            min = dom;
    }
    outputDOM[outputId] = min;
}
```

8. Finally, return the set of degrees of membership:

```
return outputDOM;
```

How it works...

We make use of the boxing/unboxing technique for handling any input via the object data type. The *fuzzification* process is done with the help of our own membership functions, derived from the base class that we created in the beginning. Then, we take the minimum degree of membership for the input state for each rule and calculate the final degree of membership for each output state given the maximum output from any of the applicable rules.

There's more...

We can create an example membership function to define whether an enemy is in enraged mode, knowing that its life points (ranging from 0 to 100) are equal to or less than 30.

The following is the code for the example `MFEnraged` class:

```
using UnityEngine;
using System;
using System.Collections;

public class MFEnraged : MembershipFunction
```

```
    {
        public override float GetDOM(object input)
        {
            if ((int)input <= 30)
                return 1f;
            return 0f;
        }
    }
```

It's worth noting that it is a common requirement to have a complete set of rules; one for each combination of states from each input. This makes the recipe lack in scalability, but it works well for a smaller number of input variables and a small number of states per variable.

See also

For more theoretical insights regarding (de)*fuzzification* and scalability weaknesses, please refer to Ian Millington's book, *Artificial Intelligence for Games*.

Representing states with numerical values: Markov system

Having learned about fuzzy logic, it may do us well to mix some approaches and probably extend the functionality with finite-state machines. However, fuzzy logic doesn't work directly with values—they have to be *defuzzified* before they have a meaning within its scope. A Markov chain is a mathematical system that allows us to develop a decision-making system that can be seen as a fuzzy state machine.

Getting ready

This recipe uses the matrix and vector classes that come with Unity to illustrate the theoretical approach and make a working example, but it can be improved with our own matrix and vector classes with the proper implementation of the required member functions, such as vector-matrix multiplication.

How to do it...

1. Create the parent class for handling transitions:

    ```
    using UnityEngine;
    using System.Collections;

    public class MarkovTransition : MonoBehaviour
    {
    ```

```
    public Matrix4x4 matrix;
    public MonoBehaviour action;
}
```

2. Implement the `IsTriggered` member function:

```
public virtual bool IsTriggered()
{
    // implementation details here
    return false;
}
```

3. Define the Markov state machine with its member variables:

```
using UnityEngine;
using System.Collections;
using System.Collections.Generic;

public class MarkovStateMachine : MonoBehaviour
{
    public Vector4 state;
    public Matrix4x4 defaultMatrix;
    public float timeReset;
    public float timeCurrent;
    public List<MarkovTransition> transitions;
    private MonoBehaviour action;
}
```

4. Define the `Start` function for initialization:

```
void Start()
{
    timeCurrent = timeReset;
}
```

5. Implement the `Update` function:

```
void Update()
{
    if (action != null)
        action.enabled = false;

    MarkovTransition triggeredTransition;
    triggeredTransition = null;
    // next steps
}
```

6. Look for a triggered transition:

```
foreach (MarkovTransition mt in transitions)
{
    if (mt.IsTriggered())
    {
        triggeredTransition = mt;
        break;
    }
}
```

7. If found, compute its matrix into the game state:

```
if (triggeredTransition != null)
{
    timeCurrent = timeReset;
    Matrix4x4 matrix = triggeredTransition.matrix;
    state = matrix * state;
    action = triggeredTransition.action;
}
```

8. Otherwise, update the countdown timer and compute the default matrix into the game state, if necessary:

```
else
{
    timeCurrent -= Time.deltaTime;
    if (timeCurrent <= 0f)
    {
        state = defaultMatrix * state;
        timeCurrent = timeReset;
        action = null;
    }
}
```

How it works...

We define a game state based on the numerical value of the vector 4 member variable, with each position corresponding to a single state. The values in the game state change according to the matrix attached to each transition. When transitions are triggered, the game state changes, but we also have a countdown timer to handle a default transition and change the game accordingly. This is useful when we need to reset the game state after a period of time or just apply a regular transformation.

For more theoretical insights regarding the Markov process' application to game AI, please refer to Ian Millington's book, *Artificial Intelligence for Games.*

Making decisions with goal-oriented behaviors

Goal-oriented behaviors are a set of techniques aimed at giving agents not only a sense of intelligence, but also a sense of free will, once a goal is defined, and given a set of rules to choose from.

Imagine that we're developing a trooper agent that needs to only reach the endpoint of capturing the flag (the main goal), while taking care of its life and ammo (the inner goals for reaching the first). One way of implementing it is by using a general-purpose algorithm for handling goals, so the agent develops something similar to free will.

Getting ready

We will learn how to create a goal-based action selector that chooses an action considering the main goal, avoids unintentional actions with disrupting effects, and takes an action's duration into account. Just like the previous recipe, this requires the modeling of goals in terms of numerical values.

How to do it...

Along with the action chooser, we will create base classes for actions and goals:

1. Create the base class for modeling actions:

```
using UnityEngine;
using System.Collections;

public class ActionGOB : MonoBehaviour
{
    public virtual float GetGoalChange(GoalGOB goal)
    {
        return 0f;
    }

    public virtual float GetDuration()
    {
        return 0f;
    }
}
```

2. Create the `GoalGOB` parent class with member functions:

```csharp
using UnityEngine;
using System.Collections;

public class GoalGOB
{
    public string name;
    public float value;
    public float change;
}
```

3. Define the proper functions to handle discontentment and change over time:

```csharp
public virtual float GetDiscontentment(float newValue)
{
    return newValue * newValue;
}

public virtual float GetChange()
{
    return 0f;
}
```

4. Define the `ActionChooser` class:

```csharp
using UnityEngine;
using System.Collections;

public class ActionChooser : MonoBehaviour
{
}
```

5. Implement the function for handling unintentional actions:

```csharp
public float CalculateDiscontentment(ActionGOB action, GoalGOB[]
goals)
{
    float discontentment = 0;
    foreach (GoalGOB goal in goals)
    {
        float newValue = goal.value + action.GetGoalChange(goal);
        newValue += action.GetDuration() * goal.GetChange();
        discontentment += goal.GetDiscontentment(newValue);
    }
    return discontentment;
}
```

6. Implement the function for choosing an action:

```
public ActionGOB Choose(ActionGOB[] actions, GoalGOB[] goals)
{
    ActionGOB bestAction;
    bestAction = actions[0];
    float bestValue = CalculateDiscontentment(actions[0], goals);
    float value;
    // next steps
}
```

7. Pick the best action based on which one is least compromising:

```
foreach (ActionGOB action in actions)
{
    value = CalculateDiscontentment(action, goals);
    if (value < bestValue)
    {
        bestValue = value;
        bestAction = action;
    }
}
```

8. Return the best action:

```
return bestAction;
```

How it works...

The discontentment functions help avoid unintended actions, depending on how much a goal's value changes, in terms of an action and the time it takes to be executed. Then, the function for choosing an action is taken care of by computing the most promising one in terms of the minimum impact (discontentment).

4
Coordination and Tactics

In this chapter, we will learn techniques for coordination and devising tactics:

- ▶ Handling formations
- ▶ Extending A* for coordination: A*mbush
- ▶ Creating good waypoints
- ▶ Analyzing waypoints by height
- ▶ Analyzing waypoints by cover and visibility
- ▶ Exemplifying waypoints for decision making
- ▶ Introducing influence maps
- ▶ Improving influence with map flooding
- ▶ Improving influence with convolution filters
- ▶ Building a fighting circle

Introduction

As we will see, this is not a chapter focused on a sole subject, but rather a chapter that has its own original recipes and also learns from previous recipes in order to create new or improved techniques.

In this chapter, we will learn different recipes for coordinating different agents into one organism, such as formations and techniques that allow us to make tactical decisions based on graphs (such as waypoints) and influence maps. These techniques use different elements from the previous chapters and recipes, especially from the graph construction and path finding algorithms found in *Chapter 2, Navigation*.

Handling formations

This is a key algorithm for creating flocks or a group of military agents. It is designed to be flexible enough to give you the chance to create your own formations.

The end result from this recipe will be a set of target positions and rotations for each agent in the formation. Then, it is up to you to create the necessary algorithms to move the agent to the previous targets.

 We can use the movement algorithms learnt in *Chapter 1, Movement*, in order to target those positions.

Getting ready

We will need to create three base classes that are the data types to be used by the high-level classes and algorithms. The Location class is very similar to the Steering class and is used to define a target position and rotation given the formation's anchor point and rotation. The SlogAssignment class is a data type to match a list's indices and agents. Finally, the Character class component holds the target Location class.

The following is the code for the Location class:

```
using UnityEngine;
using System.Collections;

public class Location
{
    public Vector3 position;
    public Quaternion rotation;

    public Location ()
    {
        position = Vector3.zero;
        rotation = Quaternion.identity;
    }

    public Location(Vector3 position, Quaternion rotation)
```

```
    {
        this.position = position;
        this.rotation = rotation;
    }
}
```

The following is the code for the SlotAssignment class:

```
using UnityEngine;
using System.Collections;

public class SlotAssignment
{
    public int slotIndex;
    public GameObject character;

    public SlotAssignment()
    {
        slotIndex = -1;
        character = null;
    }
}
```

The following is the code for the Character class:

```
using UnityEngine;
using System.Collections;

public class Character : MonoBehaviour
{
    public Location location;

    public void SetTarget (Location location)
    {
        this.location = location;
    }
}
```

How to do it...

We will implement two classes—FormationPattern and FormationManager:

1. Create the FormationPattern pseudo-abstract class:

    ```
    using UnityEngine;
    using System.Collections;
    ```

```
using System.Collections.Generic;

public class FormationPattern: MonoBehaviour
{
    public int numOfSlots;
    public GameObject leader;
}
```

2. Implement the `Start` function:

```
void Start()
{
    if (leader == null)
        leader = transform.gameObject;
}
```

3. Define the function for getting the position for a given slot:

```
public virtual Vector3 GetSlotLocation(int slotIndex)
{
    return Vector3.zero;
}
```

4. Define the function for retrieving whether a given number of slots is supported by the formation:

```
public bool SupportsSlots(int slotCount)
{
    return slotCount <= numOfSlots;
}
```

5. Implement the function for setting an offset in the locations, if necessary:

```
public virtual Location GetDriftOffset(List<SlotAssignment>
slotAssignments)
{
    Location location = new Location();
    location.position = leader.transform.position;
    location.rotation = leader.transform.rotation;
    return location;
}
```

6. Create the appropriate class for managing the formation:

```
using UnityEngine;
using System.Collections;
using System.Collections.Generic;

public class FormationManager : MonoBehaviour
{
```

```
    public FormationPattern pattern;
    private List<SlotAssignment> slotAssignments;
    private Location driftOffset;
}
```

7. Implement the `Awake` function:

```
void Awake()
{
    slotAssignments = new List<SlotAssignment>();
}
```

8. Define the function for updating the slot assignments given the list's order:

```
public void UpdateSlotAssignments()
{
    for (int i = 0; i < slotAssignments.Count; i++)
    {
        slotAssignments[i].slotIndex = i;
    }
    driftOffset = pattern.GetDriftOffset(slotAssignments);
}
```

9. Implement the function for adding a character in the formation:

```
public bool AddCharacter(GameObject character)
{
    int occupiedSlots = slotAssignments.Count;
    if (!pattern.SupportsSlots(occupiedSlots + 1))
        return false;
    SlotAssignment sa = new SlotAssignment();
    sa.character = character;
    slotAssignments.Add(sa);
    UpdateSlotAssignments();
    return true;
}
```

10. Implement the function for removing a character in the formation:

```
public void RemoveCharacter(GameObject agent)
{
    int index = slotAssignments.FindIndex(x => x.character.
Equals(agent));
    slotAssignments.RemoveAt(index);
    UpdateSlotAssignments();
}
```

11. Implement the function for updating the slots:

```
public void UpdateSlots()
{
    GameObject leader = pattern.leader;
    Vector3 anchor = leader.transform.position;
    Vector3 slotPos;
    Quaternion rotation;
    rotation = leader.transform.rotation;
    foreach (SlotAssignment sa in slotAssignments)
    {
        // next step
    }
}
```

12. Finally, implement the `foreach` loop:

```
Vector3 relPos;
slotPos = pattern.GetSlotLocation(sa.slotIndex);
relPos = anchor;
relPos += leader.transform.TransformDirection(slotPos);
Location charDrift = new Location(relPos, rotation);
Character character = sa.character.GetComponent<Character>();
character.SetTarget(charDrift);
```

How it works...

The `FormationPattern` class contains the relative positions to a given slot. For example, a child `CircleFormation` class will implement the `GetSlotLocation` class, given the number of slots and its locations over 360 degrees. It is intended to be a basic class, so it is up to the manager to add a layer for permissions and rearrangement. That way, the designer can focus on simple formation scripting, deriving from the base class.

The `FormationManager` class, as stated earlier, handles the high-level layer and arranges the locations in line with the formation's needs and permissions. The calculations are based on the leader's position and rotation, and they apply the necessary transformations given the pattern's principles.

There is more...

It is worth mentioning that the `FormationManager` and `FormationPattern` classes are intended to be components of the same object. When the leader field in the manager is set to null, the leader is the object itself. That way, we could have a different leader object in order to have a clean inspector window and class modularity.

- Refer to *Chapter 1, Movement*, the *Arriving and leaving* recipe
- For further information on drift offset and how to play with this value, please refer to Ian Millington's book, *Artificial Intelligence for Games*

Extending A* for coordination: A*mbush

After learning how to implement A* for path finding, we will now use its power and flexibility to develop some kind of coordinated behavior in order to ambush the player. This algorithm is especially useful when we want a non-expensive solution for the aforementioned problem, and one that is also easy to implement.

This recipe sets the path for every agent to be taken into account when it comes to ambushing a given vertex or point in the graph.

Getting ready

We need a special component for the agents called `Lurker`. This class will hold the paths that are to be used later in the navigation process.

The following is the code for `Lurker`:

```
using UnityEngine;
using System.Collections;
using System.Collections.Generic;

public class Lurker : MonoBehaviour
{
    [HideInInspector]
    public List<int> pathIds;
    [HideInInspector]
    public List<GameObject> pathObjs;

    void Awake()
    {
        if (pathIds == null)
            pathIds = new List<int>();
        if (pathObjs == null)
            pathObjs = new List<GameObject>();
    }
}
```

How to do it...

We will create the main function for setting the ambush path for all the agents and then the function for setting each agent's path.

1. Define the main function for the ambush:

```
public void SetPathAmbush(GameObject dstObj, List<Lurker> lurkers)
{
    Vertex dst = GetNearestVertex(dstObj.transform.position);
    foreach (Lurker l in lurkers)
    {
        Vertex src = GetNearestVertex(l.transform.position);
        l.path = AStarMbush(src, dst, l, lurkers);
    }
}
```

2. Declare the function for finding each path:

```
public List<Vertex> AStarMbush(
        Vertex src,
        Vertex dst,
        Lurker agent,
        List<Lurker> lurkers,
        Heuristic h = null)
{    // next steps
}
```

3. Declare the necessary members for handling the extra cost of computations:

```
int graphSize = vertices.Count;
float[] extra = new float[graphSize];
float[] costs = new float[graphSize];
int i;
```

4. Initialize the regular cost and the extra cost variables:

```
for (i = 0; i < graphSize; i++)
{
    extra[i] = 1f;
    costs[i] = Mathf.Infinity;
}
```

5. Add extra cost to each vertex that is contained in another agent's path:

```
foreach (Lurker l in lurkers)
{
    foreach (Vertex v in l.path)
    {
```

```
            extra[v.id] += 1f;
        }
    }
```

6. Declare and initialize the variables for computing A*:

```
Edge[] successors;
int[] previous = new int[graphSize];
for (i = 0; i < graphSize; i++)
    previous[i] = -1;
previous[src.id] = src.id;
float cost = 0;
Edge node = new Edge(src, 0);
GPWiki.BinaryHeap<Edge> frontier = new GPWiki.BinaryHeap<Edge>();
```

7. Start implementing the A* main loop:

```
frontier.Add(node);
while (frontier.Count != 0)
{
    if (frontier.Count == 0)
        return new List<GameObject>();
    // next steps
}
return new List<Vertex>();
```

8. Validate that the goal has already been reached; otherwise it's not worth computing the costs, and it would be better to continue with the usual A* algorithm:

```
node = frontier.Remove();
if (ReferenceEquals(node.vertex, dst))
    return BuildPath(src.id, node.vertex.id, ref previous);
int nodeId = node.vertex.id;
if (node.cost > costs[nodeId])
    continue;
```

9. Traverse the neighbors and check whether they have been visited:

```
successors = GetEdges(node.vertex);
foreach (Edge e in successors)
{
    int eId = e.vertex.id;
    if (previous[eId] != -1)
        continue;
    // next step
}
```

10. If they haven't been visited, add them to the frontier:

```
cost = e.cost;
cost += costs[dst.id];
cost += h(e.vertex, dst);
if (cost < costs[e.vertex.id])
{
    Edge child;
    child = new Edge(e.vertex, cost);
    costs[eId] = cost;
    previous[eId] = nodeId;
    frontier.Remove(e);
    frontier.Add(child);
}
```

How it works...

The A*mbush algorithm analyses the path of every agent and increases the cost of that node. That way, when an agent computes its path using A*, it is better to choose a different route than the one chosen by other agents, thus, creating the perception of an ambush among the target positions.

There is more...

There is an easy-to-implement improvement over the algorithm, which leads to the P-A*mbush variation. Simply ordering the lurkers' list from the closest to the farthest might provide a better result at almost no extra cost in computation. This is due to the fact that the ordering operation is handled just once, and could be easily implemented via a priority queue, and then retrieves it as a list to the main A*mbush algorithm with no extra changes.

Creating good waypoints

There are times when the number of waypoints must be reduced at a certain point during the game or just for memory constraints. In this recipe, we will learn a technique called condensation that helps us deal with this problem, forcing the waypoints to compete with each other given their assigned value.

Getting ready

In this recipe, we will deal with static member functions. It is important that we understand the use and value of static functions.

How to do it...

We will create the `Waypoint` class and add the functions for condensing the set of waypoints.

1. Create the `Waypoint` class, deriving not only from `MonoBehaviour`, but also from the `IComparer` interface:

```
using UnityEngine;
using System.Collections;
using System.Collections.Generic;

public class Waypoint : MonoBehaviour, IComparer
{
    public float value;
    public List<Waypoint> neighbours;
}
```

2. Implement the `Compare` function from the aforementioned interface:

```
public int Compare(object a, object b)
{
    Waypoint wa = (Waypoint)a;
    Waypoint wb = (Waypoint)b;
    if (wa.value == wb.value)
        return 0;
    if (wa.value < wb.value)
        return -1;
    return 1;
}
```

3. Implement the static function to compute whether an agent can move between two waypoints:

```
public static bool CanMove(Waypoint a, Waypoint b)
{
    // implement your own behaviour for
    // deciding whether an agent can move
    // easily between two waypoints
    return true;
}
```

4. Start declaring the function for condensing the waypoints:

```
public static void CondenseWaypoints(List<Waypoint> waypoints,
float distanceWeight)
{
    // next steps
}
```

5. Initialize some variables and sort the waypoints in descending order:

```
distanceWeight *= distanceWeight;
waypoints.Sort();
waypoints.Reverse();
List<Waypoint> neighbours;
```

6. Start the loop for computing each waypoint:

```
foreach (Waypoint current in waypoints)
{
    // next steps
}
```

7. Retrieve the waypoint neighbors, sort them, and start the loop to make them compete with each other:

```
neighbours = new List<Waypoint>(current.neighbours);
neighbours.Sort();
foreach (Waypoint target in neighbours)
{
    if (target.value > current.value)
        break;
    if (!CanMove(current, target))
        continue;
    // next steps
}
```

8. Compute the target's position:

```
Vector3 deltaPos = current.transform.position;
deltaPos -= target.transform.position;
deltaPos = Vector3.Cross(deltaPos, deltaPos);
deltaPos *= distanceWeight;
```

9. Compute the target's overall value and decide whether to keep it or throw it:

```
float deltaVal = current.value - target.value;
deltaVal *= deltaVal;
if (deltaVal < distanceWeight)
{
    neighbours.Remove(target);
    waypoints.Remove(target);
}
```

How it works...

The waypoints are ordered according to their relevance (such as height to be used as a sniping or advantage location) and then their neighbors are checked to see which ones are going to be dismissed from the condensation. Naturally, the less valuable waypoints are kept to the end of the computation cycle. In the next recipe, we will learn how to analyze waypoints.

See also

Refer to the the following recipes:

- ▶ *Analyzing waypoints by height*
- ▶ *Analyzing waypoints by cover and visibility*

Analyzing waypoints by height

This recipe lets us evaluate a waypoint according to its position. Strategically speaking, lower positions are at a disadvantage. In this case, we will use a flexible algorithm to get the quality of a waypoint, given the heights of its surroundings.

Getting ready

This recipe is simple enough, so there is no extra content to be aware of. The algorithm is flexible enough to receive a list of positions, which is given by the waypoint's neighbors or just the complete graph of waypoints. The surroundings heuristic is kept outside for our perusal and it gives the game's specific design.

How to do it...

We will implement a function to evaluate a location given its height and its surrounding points:

1. Declare the function for evaluating the quality:

```
public static float GetHeightQuality (Vector3 location, Vector3[]
surroundings)
{
    // next steps
}
```

2. Initialize the variables for handling the computation:

```
float maxQuality = 1f;
float minQuality = -1f;
float minHeight = Mathf.Infinity;
float maxHeight = Mathf.NegativeInfinity;
float height = location.y;
```

3. Traverse the surroundings in order to find the maximum and minimum height:

```
foreach (Vector3 s in surroundings)
{
    if (s.y > maxHeight)
        maxHeight = s.y;
    if (s.y < minHeight)
        minHeight = s.y;
}
```

4. Compute the quality in the given range:

```
float quality = (height-minHeight) / (maxHeight - minHeight);
quality *= (maxQuality - minQuality);
quality += minQuality;
return quality;
```

How it works...

We traverse the list of surroundings to find the maximum and minimum width and then compute the location value in the range of -1, 1. We could change this range to meet our game's design, or invert the importance of the height in the formula.

Analyzing waypoints by cover and visibility

When dealing with military games, especially FPS, we need to define a waypoint value, by its capacity, to be a good cover point with the maximum visibility for shooting or reaching other enemies visually. This recipe helps us compute a waypoint's value given these parameters.

Getting ready

We need to create a function for checking whether a position is in the same room as others:

```
public bool IsInSameRoom(Vector3 from, Vector3 location, string
tagWall = "Wall")
{
    RaycastHit[] hits;
    Vector3 direction = location - from;
    float rayLength = direction.magnitude;
    direction.Normalize();
    Ray ray = new Ray(from, direction);
    hits = Physics.RaycastAll(ray, rayLength);
    foreach (RaycastHit h in hits)
    {
        string tagObj = h.collider.gameObject.tag;
```

```
        if (tagObj.Equals(tagWall))
            return false;
    }
    return true;
}
```

How to do it...

We will create the function that computes the quality of the waypoint:

1. Define the function with its parameters:

```
public static float GetCoverQuality(
        Vector3 location,
        int iterations,
        Vector3 characterSize,
        float radius,
        float randomRadius,
        float deltaAngle)
{
    // next steps
}
```

2. Initialize the variable for handling the degrees of rotation, possible hits received, and valid visibility:

```
float theta = 0f;
int hits = 0;
int valid = 0;
```

3. Start the main loop for the iterations to be computed on this waypoint and return the computed value:

```
for (int i = 0; i < iterations; i++)
{
    // next steps
}
return (float)(hits / valid);
```

4. Create a random position near the waypoint's origin to see if the waypoint is easily reachable:

```
Vector3 from = location;
float randomBinomial = Random.Range(-1f, 1f);
from.x += radius * Mathf.Cos(theta) + randomBinomial *
randomRadius;
from.y += Random.value * 2f * randomRadius;
from.z += radius * Mathf.Sin(theta) + randomBinomial *
randomRadius;
```

5. Check whether the random position is in the same room:

```
if (!IsInSameRoom(from, location))
    continue;
valid++;
```

6. If the random position in the same room, then:

```
Vector3 to = location;
to.x += Random.Range(-1f, 1f) * characterSize.x;
to.y += Random.value * characterSize.y;
to.z += Random.Range(-1f, 1f) * characterSize.z;
```

7. Cast a ray to the visibility value to check whether:

```
Vector3 direction = to - location;
float distance = direction.magnitude;
direction.Normalize();
Ray ray = new Ray(location, direction);
if (Physics.Raycast(ray, distance))
    hits++;
theta = Mathf.Deg2Rad * deltaAngle;
```

How it works...

We create a number of iterations and then start putting random numbers around the waypoint to verify that it is reachable and hittable. After that, we compute a coefficient to determine its quality.

Exemplifying waypoints for decision making

Just like we learned with decision-making techniques, sometimes it is not flexible enough to just evaluate a waypoints' value, but rather a more complex condition. In this case, the solution is to apply techniques learned previously and couple them into the waypoint for attacking that problem.

The key idea is to add a condition to the node so that it can be evaluated, for example, using a decision tree and developing more complex heuristics for computing a waypoint's value.

Getting ready

It is important to revisit the recipe that handled state machines in the previous chapter before diving into the following recipe.

How to do it...

We will make a little adjustment:

1. Add `public Condition` to the `Waypoint` class:

    ```
    public Condition condition;
    ```

2. Now, you'll be able to easily integrate it into decision-making techniques using derived condition classes such as `ConditionFloat`.

How it works...

The pseudo-abstract `Condition` class, which we learned about previously, has a member function called `Test`, which evaluates whether or not that condition is met.

See also

▸ *Chapter 3, Decision Making*

Influence maps

Another way to use graphs is to represent how much reach or influence an agent, or in this case a unit, has over an area of the world. In this context, influence is represented as the total area of a map an agent, or a group of agents of the same party, covers.

This is a key element for creating good AI decision mechanisms based on the military presence in real-time simulation games, or games where it is important to know how much of the world is taken by a group of agents, each representing a given faction.

Getting ready

This is a recipe that requires the experience of graph building, so it is based on the general `Graph` class. However, we will need to derive it from a specific graph definition, or define our own methods to handle vertices and the neighbors retrieval logic, as learned in *Chapter 2, Navigation*.

We will learn how to implement the specific algorithms for this recipe, based on the `Graph` class general functions and the `Vertex` class.

Finally, we will need a base Unity component for our agent and `Faction enum`.

The following is the code for the `Faction` enum and `Unit` classes. They can be written in the same file, called `Unit.cs`:

```
using UnityEngine;
using System.Collections;

public enum Faction
{
    // example values
    BLUE, RED
}

public class Unit : MonoBehaviour
{
    public Faction faction;
    public int radius = 1;
    public float influence = 1f;

    public virtual float GetDropOff(int locationDistance)
    {
        return influence;
    }
}
```

How to do it...

We will build the `VertexInfluence` and `InfluenceMap` classes, used for handle vertices and the graph, respectively:

1. Create the `VertexInfluence` class, deriving from `Vertex`:

    ```
    using UnityEngine;
    using System.Collections.Generic;

    public class VertexInfluence : Vertex
    {
        public Faction faction;
        public float value = 0f;
    }
    ```

2. Implement the function for setting up values and notifying success:

```
public bool SetValue(Faction f, float v)
{
    bool isUpdated = false;
    if (v > value)
    {
        value = v;
        faction = f;
        isUpdated = true;
    }
    return isUpdated;
}
```

3. Create the InfluenceMap class deriving from Graph (or a more specific graph implementation):

```
using UnityEngine;
using System.Collections;
using System.Collections.Generic;

public class InfluenceMap : Graph
{
    public List<Unit> unitList;
    // works as vertices in regular graph
    GameObject[] locations;
}
```

4. Define the Awake function for initialization:

```
void Awake()
{
    if (unitList == null)
        unitList = new List<Unit>();
}
```

5. Implement the function for adding a unit on the map:

```
public void AddUnit(Unit u)
{
    if (unitList.Contains(u))
        return;
    unitList.Add(u);
}
```

6. Implement the function for removing a unit from the map:

```
public void RemoveUnit(Unit u)
{
    unitList.Remove(u);
}
```

7. Start building the function for computing the influence:

```
public void ComputeInfluenceSimple()
{
    int vId;
    GameObject vObj;
    VertexInfluence v;
    float dropOff;
    List<Vertex> pending = new List<Vertex>();
    List<Vertex> visited = new List<Vertex>();
    List<Vertex> frontier;
    Vertex[] neighbours;

    // next steps
}
```

8. Continue by creating a loop for iterating over the list of units:

```
foreach(Unit u in unitList)
{
    Vector3 uPos = u.transform.position;
    Vertex vert = GetNearestVertex(uPos);
    pending.Add(vert);

    // next step
}
```

9. Finally, apply a BFS-based code for spreading influence given the radius reach:

```
// BFS for assigning influence
for (int i = 1; i <= u.radius; i++)
{
    frontier = new List<Vertex>();
    foreach (Vertex p in pending)
    {
        if (visited.Contains(p))
            continue;
        visited.Add(p);
        v = p as VertexInfluence;
        dropOff = u.GetDropOff(i);
        v.SetValue(u.faction, dropOff);
```

```
        neighbours = GetNeighbours(vert);
        frontier.AddRange(neighbours);
    }
    pending = new List<Vertex>(frontier);
}
```

How it works...

The influence-map graph works exactly as a general graph as well as the influence-based vertex because there's just a couple of extra parameters for mapping the influence across the graph. The most relevant part relies on the computation of the influence, and it is based on the BFS algorithm.

For each unit on the map, we spread its influence given the radius. When the computed influence (drop off) is greater than the vertex original faction, the vertex faction is changed.

There is more...

The drop-off function should be tuned according to your specific game needs. We can define a smarter function with the following example code, using the distance parameter:

```
public virtual float GetDropOff(int locationDistance)
{
    float d = influence / radius * locationDistance;
    return influence - d;
}
```

It is important to note that the distance parameter is an integer indicating the distance measured in vertices.

Finally, we could avoid using factions and instead use a reference to the unit itself. That way, we could map the influence based on individual units, but we think it makes the most sense to think in terms of factions or teams.

See also

- ▸ *Chapter 2, Navigation,* the *Representing the world with grids* and *Finding the shortest path in a grid with BFS* recipes

Improving influence with map flooding

The previous influence computation is good when dealing with a simple influence that is based on individual units helping a faction. However, this could lead to holes in the map instead of covering a whole section. One technique to resolve that problem is flooding, based on the Dijkstra algorithm.

Getting ready

In this case, we will blend the faction capability for tagging a vertex, with the unit's logic for having a drop-off function, into a class called Guild. This is a component to include in the game object; one for each desired guild:

```
using UnityEngine;
using System;
using System.Collections;

public class Guild : MonoBehaviour
{
    public string guildName;
    public int maxStrength;
    public GameObject baseObject;
    [HideInInspector]
    public int strenghth

    public virtual void Awake()
    {
        strength = maxStrength;
    }
}
```

It also needs a drop-off function. However, this time we wanted to create an example using Euclidean distance:

```
public virtual float GetDropOff(float distance)
{
    float d = Mathf.Pow(1 + distance, 2f);
    return strength / d;
}
```

Finally, we will need a `GuildRecord` data type for the Dijkstra algorithm representation of a node:

1. Create the `GuildRecord` struct, deriving from the `IComparable` interface:

    ```
    using UnityEngine;
    using System.Collections;
    using System;

    public struct GuildRecord : IComparable<GuildRecord>
    {
        public Vertex location;
        public float strength;
        public Guild guild;
    }
    ```

2. Implement the `Equal` functions:

    ```
    public override bool Equals(object obj)
    {
        GuildRecord other = (GuildRecord)obj;
        return location == other.location;
    }

    public bool Equals(GuildRecord o)
    {
        return location == o.location;
    }
    ```

3. Implement the required `IComparable` functions:

    ```
    public override int GetHashCode()
    {
        return base.GetHashCode();
    }

    public int CompareTo(GuildRecord other)
    {
        if (location == other.location)
            return 0;
        // the substraction is inverse for
        // having a descending binary heap
        return (int)(other.strength - strength);
    }
    ```

How to do it...

Now, we just need to modify some files and add functionalities:

1. Include the `guild` member in the `VertexInfluence` class:

```
public Guild guild;
```

2. Include new members in the `InfluenceMap` class:

```
public float dropOffThreshold;
private  Guild[] guildList;
```

3. Also, in `InfluenceMap`, add the following line in the `Awake` function:

```
guildList = gameObject.GetComponents<Guild>();
```

4. Create the map-flooding function:

```
public List<GuildRecord> ComputeMapFlooding()
{
}
```

5. Declare the main necessary variables:

```
GPWiki.BinaryHeap<GuildRecord> open;
open = new GPWiki.BinaryHeap<GuildRecord>();
List<GuildRecord> closed;
closed = new List<GuildRecord>();
```

6. Add the initial nodes for each guild in the priority queue:

```
foreach (Guild g in guildList)
{
    GuildRecord gr = new GuildRecord();
    gr.location = GetNearestVertex(g.baseObject);
    gr.guild = g;
    gr.strength = g.GetDropOff(0f);
    open.Add(gr);
}
```

7. Create the main Dijkstra iteration and return the assignments:

```
while (open.Count != 0)
{
    // next steps here
}
return closed;
```

8. Take the first node in the queue and get its neighbors:

```
GuildRecord current;
current = open.Remove();
GameObject currObj;
currObj = GetVertexObj(current.location);
Vector3 currPos;
currPos = currObj.transform.position;
List<int> neighbours;
neighbours = GetNeighbors(current.location);
```

9. Create the loop for computing each neighbor, and put the current node in the closed list:

```
foreach (int n in neighbours)
{
    // next steps here
}
closed.Add(current);
```

10. Compute the drop off from the current vertex, and check whether it is worth trying to change the guild assigned:

```
GameObject nObj = GetVertexObj(n);
Vector3 nPos = nObj.transform.position;
float dist = Vector3.Distance(currPos, nPos);
float strength = current.guild.GetDropOff(dist);
if (strength < dropOffThreshold)
    continue;
```

11. Create an auxiliary `GuildRecord` node with the current vertex's data:

```
GuildRecord neighGR = new GuildRecord();
neighGR.location = n;
neighGR.strength = strength;
VertexInfluence vi;
vi = nObj.GetComponent<VertexInfluence>();
neighGR.guild = vi.guild;
```

12. Check the closed list and validate the time when a new assignment must be avoided:

```
if (closed.Contains(neighGR))
{
    int location = neighGR.location;
    int index = closed.FindIndex(x => x.location == location);
    GuildRecord gr = closed[index];
    if (gr.guild.name != current.guild.name
            && gr.strength < strength)
        continue;
}
```

13. Check the priority queue for the same reasons:

```
else if (open.Contains(neighGR))
{
    bool mustContinue = false;
    foreach (GuildRecord gr in open)
    {
        if (gr.Equals(neighGR))
        {
            mustContinue = true;
            break;
        }
    }
    if (mustContinue)
        continue;
}
```

14. Create a new `GuildRecord` assignment and add it to the priority queue when everything else fails:

```
else
{
    neighGR = new GuildRecord();
    neighGR.location = n;
}
neighGR.guild = current.guild;
neighGR.strength = strength;
```

15. Add it to the priority queue if necessary:

```
open.Add(neighGR);
```

How it works...

The algorithm returns the guild's assignment for every vertex. It traverses the whole graph starting from the guilds' bases and computes.

The algorithm traverses the whole graph starting from the guilds' positions. Given our previous inverse subtraction, the priority queue always starts from the strongest node and computes the assignment until it reaches a value below `dropOffThreshold`. It also checks for ways to avoid a new assignment if the conditions are not met: if the vertex value is greater than the current strength, or if the guild assignment is the same.

▶ The *Introducing influence maps* recipe

▶ Chapter 2, *Navigation*, the *Finding the shortest path with Dijkstra* recipe

Improving influence with convolution filters

Convolution filters are usually applied via image processing software, but we can use the same principles to change a grid's influence given a unit's value and its surroundings. In this recipe, we will explore a couple of algorithms to modify a grid using matrix filters.

Getting ready

It is important to have grasped the concept of influence maps before implementing this recipe, so that you can understand the context in which it is applied.

How to do it...

We will implement the `Convolve` function:

1. Declare the `Convolve` function:

```
public static void Convolve(
        float[,] matrix,
        ref float[,] source,
        ref float[,] destination)
{
    // next steps
}
```

2. Initialize the variables for handling the computations and traversal of arrays:

```
int matrixLength = matrix.GetLength(0);
int size = (int)(matrixLength - 1) / 2;
int height = source.GetLength(0);
int width = source.GetLength(1);
int I, j, k, m;
```

3. Create the first loop for iterating over the destination and source grids:

```
for (i = 0; i < width-- size; i++)
{
    for (j = 0; j < height-- size; j++)
    {
        // next steps
    }
}
```

4. Implement the second loop for iterating over the filter matrix:

```
destination[i, j] = 0f;
for (k = 0; k < matrixLength; k++)
{
    for (m = 0; m < matrixLength; m++)
    {
        int row = i + k-- size;
        int col = j + m-- size;
        float aux = source[row, col] * matrix[k,m];
        destination[i, j] += aux;
    }
}
```

How it works...

We create a new grid to be swapped with the original source grid after the application of the matrix filter on each position. Then, we iterate over each position that is to be created as a destination grid and compute its result, taking the original grid's value and applying the matrix filter to it.

It is important to note that the matrix filter must be an odd-square array for the algorithm to work as expected.

There is more...

The following ConvolveDriver function helps us iterate using the Convolve function implemented previously:

1. Declare the ConvolveDriver function:

```
public static void ConvolveDriver(
        float[,] matrix,
        ref float[,] source,
        ref float[,] destination,
        int iterations)
{
    // next steps
}
```

2. Create the auxiliary variables for holding the grids:

```
float[,] map1;
float[,] map2;
int i;
```

3. Swap the maps, regardless of whether the iterations are odd or even:

```
if (iterations % 2 == 0)
{
    map1 = source;
    map2 = destination;
}
else
{
    destination = source;
    map1 = destination;
    map2 = source;
}
```

4. Apply the previous function during the iterations and swap:

```
for (i = 0; i < iterations; i++)
{
    Convolve(matrix, ref source, ref destination);
    float[,] aux = map1;
    map1 = map2;
    map2 = aux;
}
```

See also

▸ The *Introducing influence maps* recipe

Building a fighting circle

This recipe is based on the Kung-Fu Circle algorithm devised for the game, *Kingdoms of Amalur: Reckoning*. Its purpose is to offer an intelligent way for enemies to approach a given player and set attacks on it. It is very similar to the formation recipe, but it uses a stage manager that handles approach and attack permissions based on enemy weights and attack weights. It is also implemented so that the manager has the capability to handle a list of fighting circles; this is especially aimed at multiplayer games.

Getting ready

Before implementing the fighting circle algorithm, it is important to create some components that accompany the technique. First, the Attack class is a pseudo-abstract class for creating general-purpose attacks for each enemy, and it works as a template for our custom attacks in our game. Second, we need the Enemy class, which is the holder of the enemy's logic and requests. As we will see, the Enemy class holds a list of the different attack components found in the game object.

The code for the `Attack` class is as follows:

```
using UnityEngine;
using System.Collections;

public class Attack : MonoBehaviour
{
    public int weight;

    public virtual IEnumerator Execute()
    {
        // your attack behaviour here
        yield break;
    }
}
```

The steps to build the `Enemy` component are as follows:

1. Create the `Enemy` class:

   ```
   using UnityEngine;
   using System.Collections;

   public class Enemy : MonoBehaviour
   {
       public StageManager stageManager;
       public int slotWeight;
       [HideInInspector]
       public int circleId = -1;
       [HideInInspector]
       public bool isAssigned;
       [HideInInspector]
       public bool isAttacking;
       [HideInInspector]
       public Attack[] attackList;
   }
   ```

2. Implement the `Start` function:

   ```
   void Start()
   {
       attackList = gameObject.GetComponents<Attack>();
   }
   ```

3. Implement the function for assigning a target fighting circle:

```
public void SetCircle(GameObject circleObj = null)
{
    int id = -1;
    if (circleObj == null)
    {
        Vector3 position = transform.position;
        id = stageManager.GetClosestCircle(position);
    }
    else
    {
        FightingCircle fc;
        fc = circleObj.GetComponent<FightingCircle>();
        if (fc != null)
            id = fc.gameObject.GetInstanceID();
    }
    circleId = id;
}
```

4. Define the function for requesting a slot to the manager:

```
public bool RequestSlot()
{
    isAssigned = stageManager.GrantSlot(circleId, this);
    return isAssigned;
}
```

5. Define the function for releasing the slot from the manager:

```
public void ReleaseSlot()
{
    stageManager.ReleaseSlot(circleId, this);
    isAssigned = false;
    circleId = -1;
}
```

6. Implement the function for requesting an attack from the list (the order is the same from the Inspector):

```
public bool RequestAttack(int id)
{
    return stageManager.GrantAttack(circleId, attackList[id]);
}
```

7. Define the virtual function for the attack behavior:

```
public virtual IEnumerator Attack()
{
    // TODO
    // your attack behaviour here
    yield break;
}
```

How to do it...

Now, we implement the FightingCircle and StageManager classes

1. Create the FightingCircle class along with its member variables:

```
using UnityEngine;
using System.Collections;
using System.Collections.Generic;

public class FightingCircle : MonoBehaviour
{
    public int slotCapacity;
    public int attackCapacity;
    public float attackRadius;
    public GameObject player;
    [HideInInspector]
    public int slotsAvailable;
    [HideInInspector]
    public int attackAvailable;
    [HideInInspector]
    public List<GameObject> enemyList;
    [HideInInspector]
    public Dictionary<int, Vector3> posDict;
}
```

2. Implement the Awake function for initialization:

```
void Awake()
{
    slotsAvailable = slotCapacity;
    attackAvailable = attackCapacity;
    enemyList = new List<GameObject>();
    posDict = new Dictionary<int, Vector3>();
    if (player == null)
        player = gameObject;
}
```

3. Define the `Update` function so that the slots' positions get updated:

```
void Update()
{
    if (enemyList.Count == 0)
        return;
    Vector3 anchor = player.transform.position;
    int i;
    for (i = 0; i < enemyList.Count; i++)
    {
        Vector3 position = anchor;
        Vector3 slotPos = GetSlotLocation(i);
        int enemyId = enemyList[i].GetInstanceID();
        position += player.transform.TransformDirection(slotPos);
        posDict[enemyId] = position;
    }
}
```

4. Implement the function for adding enemies to the circle:

```
public bool AddEnemy(GameObject enemyObj)
{
    Enemy enemy = enemyObj.GetComponent<Enemy>();
    int enemyId = enemyObj.GetInstanceID();
    if (slotsAvailable < enemy.slotWeight)
        return false;
    enemyList.Add(enemyObj);
    posDict.Add(enemyId, Vector3.zero);
    slotsAvailable -= enemy.slotWeight;
    return true;
}
```

5. Implement the function for removing enemies from the circle:

```
public bool RemoveEnemy(GameObject enemyObj)
{
    bool isRemoved = enemyList.Remove(enemyObj);
    if (isRemoved)
    {
        int enemyId = enemyObj.GetInstanceID();
        posDict.Remove(enemyId);
        Enemy enemy = enemyObj.GetComponent<Enemy>();
        slotsAvailable += enemy.slotWeight;
    }
    return isRemoved;
}
```

6. Implement the function for swapping enemy positions in the circle:

```
public void SwapEnemies(GameObject enemyObjA, GameObject
enemyObjB)
{
    int indexA = enemyList.IndexOf(enemyObjA);
    int indexB = enemyList.IndexOf(enemyObjB);
    if (indexA != -1 && indexB != -1)
    {
        enemyList[indexB] = enemyObjA;
        enemyList[indexA] = enemyObjB;
    }
}
```

7. Define the function for getting an enemy's spatial position according to the circle:

```
public Vector3? GetPositions(GameObject enemyObj)
{
    int enemyId = enemyObj.GetInstanceID();
    if (!posDict.ContainsKey(enemyId))
        return null;
    return posDict[enemyId];
}
```

8. Implement the function for computing the spatial location of a slot:

```
private Vector3 GetSlotLocation(int slot)
{
    Vector3 location = new Vector3();
    float degrees = 360f / enemyList.Count;
    degrees *= (float)slot;
    location.x = Mathf.Cos(Mathf.Deg2Rad * degrees);
    location.x *= attackRadius;
    location.z = Mathf.Cos(Mathf.Deg2Rad * degrees);
    location.z *= attackRadius;
    return location;
}
```

9. Implement the function for virtually adding attacks to the circle:

```
public bool AddAttack(int weight)
{
    if (attackAvailable - weight < 0)
        return false;
    attackAvailable -= weight;
    return true;
}
```

10. Define the function for virtually releasing the attacks from the circle:

```
public void ResetAttack()
{
    attackAvailable = attackCapacity;
}
```

11. Now, create the StageManager class:

```
using UnityEngine;
using System.Collections;
using System.Collections.Generic;

public class StageManager : MonoBehaviour
{
    public List<FightingCircle> circleList;
    private Dictionary<int, FightingCircle> circleDic;
    private Dictionary<int, List<Attack>> attackRqsts;
}
```

12. Implement the Awake function for initialization:

```
void Awake()
{
    circleList = new List<FightingCircle>();
    circleDic = new Dictionary<int, FightingCircle>();
    attackRqsts = new Dictionary<int, List<Attack>>();
    foreach(FightingCircle fc in circleList)
    {
        AddCircle(fc);
    }
}
```

13. Create the function for adding circles to the manager:

```
public void AddCircle(FightingCircle circle)
{
    if (!circleList.Contains(circle))
        return;
    circleList.Add(circle);
    int objId = circle.gameObject.GetInstanceID();
    circleDic.Add(objId, circle);
    attackRqsts.Add(objId, new List<Attack>());
}
```

14. Also, create the function for removing circles from the manager:

```
public void RemoveCircle(FightingCircle circle)
{
    bool isRemoved = circleList.Remove(circle);
    if (!isRemoved)
        return;
    int objId = circle.gameObject.GetInstanceID();
    circleDic.Remove(objId);
    attackRqsts[objId].Clear();
    attackRqsts.Remove(objId);
}
```

15. Define the function for getting the closest circle, if given a position:

```
public int GetClosestCircle(Vector3 position)
{
    FightingCircle circle = null;
    float minDist = Mathf.Infinity;
    foreach(FightingCircle c in circleList)
    {
        Vector3 circlePos = c.transform.position;
        float dist = Vector3.Distance(position, circlePos);
        if (dist < minDist)
        {
            minDist = dist;
            circle = c;
        }
    }
    return circle.gameObject.GetInstanceID();
}
```

16. Define the function for granting an enemy a slot in a given circle:

```
public bool GrantSlot(int circleId, Enemy enemy)
{
    return circleDic[circleId].AddEnemy(enemy.gameObject);
}
```

17. Implement the function for releasing an enemy from a given circle ID:

```
public void ReleaseSlot(int circleId, Enemy enemy)
{
    circleDic[circleId].RemoveEnemy(enemy.gameObject);
}
```

18. Define the function for granting attack permissions and adding them to the manager:

```
public bool GrantAttack(int circleId, Attack attack)
{
    bool answer = circleDic[circleId].AddAttack(attack.weight);
    attackRqsts[circleId].Add(attack);
    return answer;
}
```

19. Step:

```
public IEnumerator ExecuteAtacks()
{
    foreach (int circle in attackRqsts.Keys)
    {
        List<Attack> attacks = attackRqsts[circle];
        foreach (Attack a in attacks)
            yield return a.Execute();
    }
    foreach (FightingCircle fc in circleList)
        fc.ResetAttack();
}
```

How it works...

The Attack and Enemy classes control the behaviors when needed, so the Enemy class can be called from another component in the game object. The FightingCircle class is very similar to FormationPattern, in that it computes the target positions for a given enemy. It just does it in a slightly different way. Finally, the StageManager grants all the necessary permissions for assigning and releasing enemy and attack slots for each circle.

There is more...

It is worth noting that the fighting circle can be added as a component of a game object that works as the target player itself, or a different empty object that holds a reference to the player's game object.

Also, you could move the functions for granting and executing attacks to the fighting circle. We wanted to keep them in the manager so that attack executions are centralized, and the circles just handle target positions, just like formations.

See also

- ▶ Refer to the *Handling formations* recipe
- ▶ For further information on the Kung-Fu Circle algorithm, please refer to the book, *Game AI Pro*, by Steve Rabin

5

Agent Awareness

In this chapter, we will learn some algorithm recipes for simulating senses and agent awareness:

- ▶ The seeing function using a collider-based system
- ▶ The hearing function using a collider-based system
- ▶ The smelling function using a collider-based system
- ▶ The seeing function using a graph-based system
- ▶ The hearing function using a graph-based system
- ▶ The smelling function using a graph-based system
- ▶ Creating awareness in a stealth game

Introduction

In this chapter, we will learn different approaches on how to simulate sense stimuli on an agent. We will learn how to use tools that we are already familiar with to create these simulations: colliders, and graphs.

On the first approach, we will take advantage of ray casting, colliders, and the MonoBehaviour functions bound to this component, such as `OnCollisionEnter`, in order to leverage the need to acquire objects nearby in the three-dimensional world. Then, we will learn how to simulate the same stimuli using the graph theory and functions so that we can take advantage of this way of representing the world.

Finally, we'll learn how to implement agent awareness using a mixed approach that considers the previously learned sensory-level algorithms.

The seeing function using a collider-based system

This is probably the easiest way to simulate vision. We take a collider, be it a mesh or a Unity primitive, and use it as the tool for determining whether or not an object is inside the agent's vision range.

Getting ready

It's important to have a collider component attached to the same game object using the script on this recipe, as well as the other collider-based algorithms in this chapter. In this case, it's recommended that the collider is a pyramid-based one in order to simulate a vision cone. The fewer the polygons, the faster it will be in the game.

How to do it...

We will create a component that is able to see enemies nearby:

1. Create the `Visor` component declaring its member variables. It is important to add the following corresponding tags into Unity's configuration:

```
using UnityEngine;
using System.Collections;

public class Visor : MonoBehaviour
{
    public string tagWall = "Wall";
    public string tagTarget = "Enemy";
    public GameObject agent;
}
```

2. Implement the function for initializing the game object in case the component is already assigned to it:

```
void Start()
{
    if (agent == null)
        agent = gameObject;
}
```

3. Declare the function for checking collisions in every frame, and let's build it in the following steps:

```
public void OnTriggerStay(Collider coll)
{
    // next steps here
}
```

4. Discard the collision if it is not a target:

```
string tag = coll.gameObject.tag;
if (!tag.Equals(tagTarget))
    return;
```

5. Get the game object's position and compute its direction from the visor:

```
GameObject target = coll.gameObject;
Vector3 agentPos = agent.transform.position;
Vector3 targetPos = target.transform.position;
Vector3 direction = targetPos - agentPos;
```

6. Compute its length and create a new ray to be shot soon:

```
float length = direction.magnitude;
direction.Normalize();
Ray ray = new Ray(agentPos, direction);
```

7. Cast the created ray and retrieve all the hits:

```
RaycastHit[] hits;
hits = Physics.RaycastAll(ray, length);
```

8. Check for any wall between the visor and target. If none, we can proceed to call our functions or develop our behaviors that are to be triggered:

```
int i;
for (i = 0; i < hits.Length; i++)
{
    GameObject hitObj;
    hitObj = hits[i].collider.gameObject;
    tag = hitObj.tag;
    if (tag.Equals(tagWall))
        return;
}
// TODO
// target is visible
// code your behaviour below
```

How it works...

The collider component checks every frame if it is colliding with any game object in the scene. We leverage the optimizations to Unity's scene graph and engine, and focus only on how to handle the valid collisions.

After checking, if a target object is inside the vision range represented by the collider, we cast a ray in order to check whether it is really visible or if there is a wall in between.

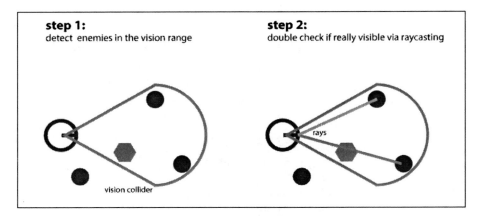

The hearing function using a collider-based system

In this recipe, we will emulate the sense of hearing by developing two entities: a sound emitter and a sound receiver. It is based on the principles proposed by Millington for simulating a hearing system, and it uses the power of Unity colliders to detect receivers near an emitter.

Getting ready

As with the other recipes based on colliders, we will need collider components attached to every object that is to be checked, and rigid body components attached to either emitters or receivers.

How to do it...

We will create the SoundReceiver class for our agents, and SoundEmitter for things such as alarms:

1. Create the class for the sound-receiver object:

```
using UnityEngine;
using System.Collections;

public class SoundReceiver : MonoBehaviour
{
    public float soundThreshold;
}
```

2. Define the function for our own behavior that is handling the reception of sound:

```
public virtual void Receive(float intensity, Vector3 position)
{
    // TODO
    // code your own behaviour here
}
```

3. Now, let's create the class for the sound-emitter object:

```
using UnityEngine;
using System.Collections;
using System.Collections.Generic;

public class SoundEmitter : MonoBehaviour
{
    public float soundIntensity;
    public float soundAttenuation;
    public GameObject emitterObject;
    private Dictionary<int, SoundReceiver> receiverDic;
}
```

4. Initialize the list of nearby receivers and the emitter object, in case the component is attached directly:

```
void Start()
{
    receiverDic = new Dictionary<int, SoundReceiver>();
    if (emitterObject == null)
        emitterObject = gameObject;
}
```

5. Implement the function for adding new receivers to the list when they enter the emitter bounds:

```
public void OnTriggerEnter(Collider coll)
{
    SoundReceiver receiver;
    receiver = coll.gameObject.GetComponent<SoundReceiver>();
    if (receiver == null)
        return;
    int objId = coll.gameObject.GetInstanceID();
    receiverDic.Add(objId, receiver);
}
```

6. Also, implement the function for removing receivers from the list when they are out of reach:

```
public void OnTriggerExit(Collider coll)
{
    SoundReceiver receiver;
    receiver = coll.gameObject.GetComponent<SoundReceiver>();
    if (receiver == null)
        return;
    int objId = coll.gameObject.GetInstanceID();
    receiverDic.Remove(objId);
}
```

7. Define the function for emitting sound waves to nearby agents:

```
public void Emit()
{
    GameObject srObj;
    Vector3 srPos;
    float intensity;
    float distance;
    Vector3 emitterPos = emitterObject.transform.position;
    // next step here
}
```

8. Compute sound attenuation for every receiver:

```
foreach (SoundReceiver sr in receiverDic.Values)
{
    srObj = sr.gameObject;
    srPos = srObj.transform.position;
    distance = Vector3.Distance(srPos, emitterPos);
    intensity = soundIntensity;
    intensity -= soundAttenuation * distance;
    if (intensity < sr.soundThreshold)
        continue;
    sr.Receive(intensity, emitterPos);
}
```

How it works...

The collider triggers help register agents in the list of agents assigned to an emitter. The sound emission function then takes into account the agent's distance from the emitter in order to decrease its intensity using the concept of sound attenuation.

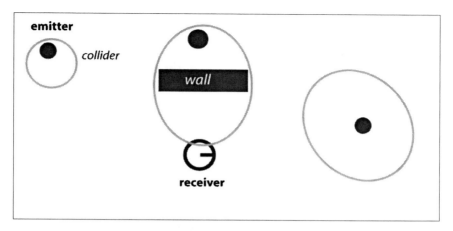

There is more...

We can develop a more flexible algorithm by defining different types of walls that affect sound intensity. It works by casting rays and adding up their values to the sound attenuation:

1. Create a dictionary for storing wall types as strings (using tags), and their corresponding attenuation:

```
public Dictionary<string, float> wallTypes;
```

2. Reduce sound intensity this way:

```
intensity -= GetWallAttenuation(emitterPos, srPos);
```

3. Define the function that was called in the previous step:

```
public float GetWallAttenuation(Vector3 emitterPos, Vector3 receiverPos)
{
    // next steps here
}
```

4. Compute the necessary values for ray casting:

```
float attenuation = 0f;
Vector3 direction = receiverPos - emitterPos;
float distance = direction.magnitude;
direction.Normalize();
```

5. Cast the ray and retrieve the hits:

```
Ray ray = new Ray(emitterPos, direction);
RaycastHit[] hits = Physics.RaycastAll(ray, distance);
```

6. For every wall type found via tags, add up its value (stored in the dictionary):

```
int i;
for (i = 0; i < hits.Length; i++)
{
    GameObject obj;
    string tag;
    obj = hits[i].collider.gameObject;
    tag = obj.tag;
    if (wallTypes.ContainsKey(tag))
        attenuation += wallTypes[tag];
}
return attenuation;
```

The smelling function using a collider-based system

Smelling is one of the trickiest senses to translate from the real to the virtual world. There are several techniques, but most of them are inclined to the use of colliders or graph logic.

Smelling can be simulated by computing a collision between an agent and odor particles scattered throughout the game level.

Getting ready

As with the other recipes based on colliders, we will need collider components attached to every object that is to be checked, and rigid body components attached to either emitters or receivers.

How to do it...

We will develop the scripts for representing odor particles and agents that are able to smell:

1. Create the particle's script and define its member variables for computing its lifespan:

```
using UnityEngine;
using System.Collections;

public class OdourParticle : MonoBehaviour
{
    public float timespan;
    private float timer;
}
```

2. Implement the `Start` function for proper validations:

```
void Start()
{
    if (timespan < 0f)
        timespan = 0f;
    timer = timespan;
}
```

3. Implement the timer and destroy the object after its lifecycle:

```
void Update()
{
    timer -= Time.deltaTime;
    if (timer < 0f)
        Destroy(gameObject);
}
```

4. Create the class for representing the sniffer agent:

```
using UnityEngine;
using System.Collections;
using System.Collections.Generic;

public class Smeller : MonoBehaviour
{
    private Vector3 target;
    private Dictionary<int, GameObject> particles;
}
```

5. Initialize the dictionary for storing odor particles:

```
void Start()
{
    particles = new Dictionary<int, GameObject>();
}
```

6. Add to the dictionary the colliding objects that have the odor-particle component attached:

```
public void OnTriggerEnter(Collider coll)
{
    GameObject obj = coll.gameObject;
    OdourParticle op;
    op = obj.GetComponent<OdourParticle>();
    if (op == null)
        return;
    int objId = obj.GetInstanceID();
    particles.Add(objId, obj);
    UpdateTarget();
}
```

7. Release the odor particles from the local dictionary when they are out of the agent's range or are destroyed:

```
public void OnTriggerExit(Collider coll)
{
    GameObject obj = coll.gameObject;
    int objId = obj.GetInstanceID();
    bool isRemoved;
    isRemoved = particles.Remove(objId);
    if (!isRemoved)
        return;
    UpdateTarget();
}
```

8. Create the function for computing the odor centroid according to the current elements in the dictionary:

```
private void UpdateTarget()
{
    Vector3 centroid = Vector3.zero;
    foreach (GameObject p in particles.Values)
    {
        Vector3 pos = p.transform.position;
        centroid += pos;
    }
    target = centroid;
}
```

9. Implement the function for retrieving the odor centroids, if any:

```
public Vector3? GetTargetPosition()
{
    if (particles.Keys.Count == 0)
        return null;
    return target;
}
```

How it works...

Just like the hearing recipe based on colliders, we use the trigger colliders in order to register odor particles in an agent's perception (implemented using a dictionary). When a particle is included or removed, the odor centroid is computed. However, we implement a function for retrieving that centroid because when no odor particle is registered, the internal centroid position is not updated.

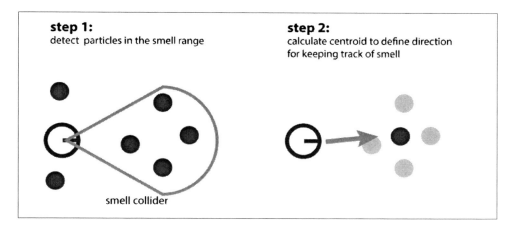

step 1:
detect particles in the smell range

step 2:
calculate centroid to define direction for keeping track of smell

smell collider

There is more...

Particle emission logic is left behind to be implemented according to our game's needs, and it's basically instantiating odor-particle prefabs. Also, it is recommended that you attach the rigid-body components to the agents. Odor particles are prone to be massively instantiated, reducing the game's performance.

The seeing function using a graph-based system

We will start the recipes oriented to use graph-based logic in order to simulate sense. Again, we start by developing the sense of vision.

Getting ready

It is important to have grasped the chapter regarding path finding in order to understand the inner workings of the graph-based recipes.

How to do it...

We will just implement a new file:

1. Create the class for handling vision:
   ```
   using UnityEngine;
   using System.Collections;
   ```

```
using System.Collections.Generic;

public class VisorGraph : MonoBehaviour
{
    public int visionReach;
    public GameObject visorObj;
    public Graph visionGraph;
}
```

2. Validate the visor object in case the com:

```
void Start()
{
    if (visorObj == null)
        visorObj = gameObject;
}
```

3. Define and start building the function for detecting the visibility of a given set of nodes:

```
public bool IsVisible(int[] visibilityNodes)
{
    int vision = visionReach;
    int src = visionGraph.GetNearestVertex(visorObj);
    HashSet<int> visibleNodes = new HashSet<int>();
    Queue<int> queue = new Queue<int>();
    queue.Enqueue(src);
}
```

4. Implement a Breadth-First Search algorithm:

```
while (queue.Count != 0)
{
    if (vision == 0)
        break;
    int v = queue.Dequeue();
    List<int> neighbours = visionGraph.GetNeighbors(v);
    foreach (int n in neighbours)
    {
        if (visibleNodes.Contains(n))
            continue;
        queue.Enqueue(v);
        visibleNodes.Add(v);
    }
}
```

5. Compare the set of visible nodes with the set of nodes reached by the vision system:

```
foreach (int vn in visibleNodes)
{
    if (visibleNodes.Contains(vn))
        return true;
}
```

6. Return false if there is no match between the two sets of nodes:

```
return false;
```

How it works...

The recipe uses the Breadth-First Search algorithm in order to discover nodes within its vision reach, and then compares this set of nodes to the set where agents reside.

The input array is computed outside, and it's out of the scope of this recipe because it relies on pinpointing, for example, the position of each agent or object that needs to be checked visibly.

The hearing function using a graph-based system

Hearing works similarly to vision but doesn't take into account the nodes direct visibility because of the properties of the sound. However, we still need a sound receiver in order to make it work. Instead of making an agent a direct sound receiver, in this recipe, the sound travels along the sound graph and is perceived by the graph nodes.

Getting ready

It is important to have grasped the chapter regarding path finding in order to understand the inner workings of the graph-based recipes.

How to do it...

1. Create the emitter class:

```
using UnityEngine;
using System.Collections;
using System.Collections.Generic;

public class EmitterGraph : MonoBehaviour
{
    // next steps
}
```

2. Declare the member variables:

    ```
    public int soundIntensity;
    public Graph soundGraph;
    public GameObject emitterObj;
    ```

3. Implement the validation of the emitter object's reference:

    ```
    public void Start()
    {
        if (emitterObj == null)
            emitterObj = gameObject;
    }
    ```

4. Declare the function for emitting sounds:

    ```
    public int[] Emit()
    {
        // next steps
    }
    ```

5. Declare and assign the variables needed:

    ```
    List<int> nodeIds = new List<int>();
    Queue<int> queue = new Queue<int>();
    List<int> neighbours;
    int intensity = soundIntensity;
    int src = soundGraph.GetNearestVertex(emitterObj);
    ```

6. Add the source node to the list of reached nodes and the queue:

    ```
    nodeIds.Add(src);
    queue.Enqueue(src);
    ```

7. Code the Breadth-First Search loop for reaching out to nodes:

    ```
    while (queue.Count != 0)
    {
        // next steps
    }
    return nodeIds.ToArray();
    ```

8. Finish the loop if the sound runs out of intensity:

    ```
    if (intensity == 0)
        break;
    ```

9. Take a node from the queue and get its neighbors:

    ```
    int v = queue.Dequeue();
    neighbours = soundGraph.GetNeighbors(v);
    ```

10. Check the neighbors and add them to the queue if necessary:

```
foreach (int n in neighbours)
{
    if (nodeIds.Contains(n))
        continue;
    queue.Enqueue(n);
    nodeIds.Add(n);
}
```

11. Reduce the sound intensity:

```
intensity--;
```

How it works...

The recipe returns the list of affected nodes by the sound intensity using the Breadth-First Search algorithm. The algorithm stops when there are no more nodes to visit, or when the intensity of the sound is dimmed by the graph traversal.

There is more...

After learning how to implement hearing using both colliders and graph logic, you could develop a new hybrid algorithm that relies on a heuristic that takes distance as inputs. If a node goes beyond the sound's maximum distance, there's no need to add its neighbors to the queue.

See also

The following recipes of *Chapter 2, Navigation*:

▶ *Breadth-First Search algorithm*

▶ *A* algorithm (for taking a heuristic function as argument)*

The smelling function using a graph-based system

In this recipe, we take a mixed approach to tag vertices with a given odor particle that collides with it.

Getting ready

The vertices should have a broad collider attached so that they catch the odor particles nearby.

How to do it...

1. Add the following member variable to the odor-particle script to store its parent ID:

```
public int parent;
```

2. Create the new odor-enabled class, deriving from the original vertex:

```
using UnityEngine;
using System.Collections;
using System.Collections.Generic;

public class VertexOdour : Vertex
{
    private Dictionary<int, OdourParticle> odourDic;
}
```

3. Initialize the odor dictionary in the proper function:

```
public void Start()
{
    odourDic = new Dictionary<int, OdourParticle>();
}
```

4. Add the odor to the vertex's dictionary:

```
public void OnCollisionEnter(Collision coll)
{
    OdourOdourParticle op;
    op = coll.gameObject.GetComponent<OdourParticle>();
    if (op == null)
        return;
    int id = op.parent;
    odourDic.Add(id, op);
}
```

5. Remove the odor from the vertex's dictionary:

```
public void OnCollisionExit(Collision coll)
{
    OdourParticle op;
    op = coll.gameObject.GetComponent<OdourParticle>();
    if (op == null)
        return;
    int id = op.parent;
    odourDic.Remove(id);
}
```

6. Implement the function for checking if there is any odor tagged:

```
public bool HasOdour()
{
    if (odourDic.Values.Count == 0)
        return false;
    return true;
}
```

7. Implement the function for checking if a given type of odor is indexed in the vertex:

```
public bool OdourExists(int id)
{
    return odourDic.ContainsKey(id);
}
```

How it works...

The odor particles collide with the vertices, being indexed in their odor dictionary. From that point on, our agents can check whether a given odor is registered in a vertex nearby.

See also

▸ *Chapter 2, Navigation* recipe, *BFS and graph construction*

Creating awareness in a stealth game

Now that we know how to implement sensory-level algorithms, it's time to see how they could be taken into account in order to develop higher-level techniques for creating agent awareness.

This recipe is based on the work of Brook Miles and its team at Klei Entertainment for the game, *Mark of the Ninja*. The mechanism moves around the notion of having interest sources that can be seen or heard by the agents, and a sensory manager handling them.

Getting ready

As a lot of things move around the idea of interests, we'll need two data structures for defining an interest's sense and priority, and a data type for the interest itself.

This is the data structure for sense:

```
public enum InterestSense
{
    SOUND,
    SIGHT
};
```

This is the data structure for priority:

```
public enum InterestPriority
{
    LOWEST = 0,
    BROKEN = 1,
    MISSING = 2,
    SUSPECT = 4,
    SMOKE = 4,
    BOX = 5,
    DISTRACTIONFLARE = 10,
    TERROR = 20
};
```

The following is the interest data type:

```
using UnityEngine;
using System.Collections;

public struct Interest
{
    public InterestSense sense;
    public InterestPriority priority;
    public Vector3 position;
}
```

Before developing the necessary classes for implementing this idea, it's important to note that sensory-level functions are left blank in order to keep the recipe flexible and open to our custom implementations. These implementations could be developed using some of the previously learned recipes.

How to do it...

This is a long recipe where we'll implement two extensive classes. It is advised to carefully read the following steps:

1. Let's start by creating the class that defines our agents, and its member variables:

```
using UnityEngine;
using System.Collections;
using System.Collections.Generic;

public class AgentAwared : MonoBehaviour
{
    protected Interest interest;
    protected bool isUpdated = false;
}
```

2. Define the function for checking whether a given interest is relevant or not:

```
public bool IsRelevant(Interest i)
{
    int oldValue = (int)interest.priority;
    int newValue = (int)i.priority;
    if (newValue <= oldValue)
        return false;
    return true;
}
```

3. Implement the function for setting a new interest in the agent:

```
public void Notice(Interest i)
{
    StopCoroutine(Investigate());
    interest = i;
    StartCoroutine(Investigate());
}
```

4. Define the custom function for investigating. This will have our own implementation, and it will take into account the agent's interest:

```
public virtual IEnumerator Investigate()
{
    // TODO
    // develop your implementation
    yield break;
}
```

5. Define the custom function for leading. This will define what an agent does when it's in charge of giving orders, and will depend on our own implementation:

```
public virtual IEnumerator Lead()
{
    // TODO
    // develop your implementation
    yield break;
}
```

6. Create the class for defining interest sources:

```
using UnityEngine;
using System.Collections;
using System.Collections.Generic;

public class InterestSource : MonoBehaviour
{
    public InterestSense sense;
    public float radius;
    public InterestPriority priority;
    public bool isActive;
}
```

7. Implement a property for retrieving its interest:

```
public Interest interest
{
    get
    {
        Interest i;
        i.position = transform.position;
        i.priority = priority;
        i.sense = sense;
        return i;
    }
}
```

8. Define the function for checking whether or not the agent is affected by the interest source. This could be defined in the agent's class, but it requires some changes in some of the next steps. This is one of the sensory-level functions:

```
protected bool IsAffectedSight(AgentAwared agent)
{
    // TODO
    // your sight check implementation
    return false;
}
```

9. Implement the next sensory-level function for checking if an agent is affected by sound. It has the same architectural considerations as the previous step:

```
protected bool IsAffectedSound(AgentAwared agent)
{
    // TODO
    // your sound check implementation
    return false;
}
```

10. Define the function for getting the list of agents affected by the interest source. It is declared virtual, in case we need to specify further, or simply change the way it works:

```
public virtual List<AgentAwared> GetAffected(AgentAwared[]
agentList)
{
    List<AgentAwared> affected;
    affected = new List<AgentAwared>();
    Vector3 interPos = transform.position;
    Vector3 agentPos;
    float distance;
    // next steps
}
```

11. Start creating the main loop for traversing the list of agents and return the list of affected ones:

```
foreach (AgentAwared agent in agentList)
{
    // next steps
}
return affected;
```

12. Discriminate an agent if it is out of the source's action radius:

```
agentPos = agent.transform.position;
distance = Vector3.Distance(interPos, agentPos);
if (distance > radius)
    continue;
```

13. Check whether the agent is affected, given the source's type of sense:

```
bool isAffected = false;
switch (sense)
{
    case InterestSense.SIGHT:
        isAffected = IsAffectedSight(agent);
        break;
    case InterestSense.SOUND:
```

```
            isAffected = IsAffectedSound(agent);
            break;
    }
```

14. If the agent is affected, add it to the list:

```
if (!isAffected)
    continue;
affected.Add(agent);
```

15. Next, create the class for the sensory manager:

```
using UnityEngine;
using System.Collections;
using System.Collections.Generic;

public class SensoryManager : MonoBehaviour
{
    public List<AgentAwared> agents;
    public List<InterestSource> sources;
}
```

16. Implement its Awake function:

```
public void Awake()
{
    agents = new List<AgentAwared>();
    sources = new List<InterestSource>();
}
```

17. Declare the function for getting a set of scouts, given a group of agents:

```
public List<AgentAwared> GetScouts(AgentAwared[] agents, int
leader = -1)
{
    // next steps
}
```

18. Validate according to the number of agents:

```
if (agents.Length == 0)
    return new List<AgentAwared>(0);
if (agents.Length == 1)
    return new List<AgentAwared>(agents);
```

19. Remove the leader, if given its index:

```
List<AgentAwared> agentList;
agentList = new List<AgentAwared>(agents);
if (leader > -1)
    agentList.RemoveAt(leader);
```

20. Calculate the number of scouts to retrieve:

```
List<AgentAwared> scouts;
scouts = new List<AgentAwared>();
float numAgents = (float)agents.Length;
int numScouts = (int)Mathf.Log(numAgents, 2f);
```

21. Get random scouts from the list of agents:

```
while (numScouts != 0)
{
    int numA = agentList.Count;
    int r = Random.Range(0, numA);
    AgentAwared a = agentList[r];
    scouts.Add(a);
    agentList.RemoveAt(r);
    numScouts--;
}
```

22. Retrieve the scouts:

```
return scouts;
```

23. Define the function for checking the list of interest sources:

```
public void UpdateLoop()
{
    List<AgentAwared> affected;
    AgentAwared leader;
    List<AgentAwared> scouts;
    foreach (InterestSource source in sources)
    {
        // next steps
    }
}
```

24. Avoid inactive sources:

```
if (!source.isActive)
    continue;
source.isActive = false;
```

25. Avoid sources that don't affect any agent:

```
affected = source.GetAffected(agents.ToArray());
if (affected.Count == 0)
    continue;
```

26. Get a random leader and the set of scouts:

```
int l = Random.Range(0, affected.Count);
leader = affected[l];
scouts = GetScouts(affected.ToArray(), l);
```

27. Call the leader to its role if necessary:

```
if (leader.Equals(scouts[0]))
    StartCoroutine(leader.Lead());
```

28. Finally, inform the scouts about noticing the interest, in case it's relevant to them:

```
foreach (AgentAwared a in scouts)
{
    Interest i = source.interest;
    if (a.IsRelevant(i))
        a.Notice(i);
}
```

How it works...

There is a list of interest sources that could get the attention of a number of agents in the world. Those lists are kept in a manager that handles the global update for every source, taking into account only the active ones.

An interest source receives the list of agents in the world and retrieves only the affected agents after a two-step process. First, it sets aside all the agents that are outside its action radius and then only takes into account those agents that can be reached with a finer (and more expensive) sensory-level mechanism.

The manager handles the affected agents, sets up a leader and scouts, and finally

There is more...

It is worth mentioning that the SensoryManager class works as a hub to store and organize the list of agents and the list of interest sources, so it ought to be a singleton. Its duplication could bring undesired complexity or behavior.

An agent's interest is automatically changed by the sensory manager using the priority values. Still, it can be reset when needed, using the public function Notice.

There is room for improvement still, depending on our game. The scout lists can overlap with each other, and it's up to us and our game to handle this scenario the best way we can. However, the system we built takes advantage of the priority values to make decisions.

See also

For further information on the train of thought behind this recipe, please refer to Steve Rabin's book, *Game AI Pro*.

6
Board Games AI

In this chapter, you will learn a family of algorithms for developing AI for board games:

- ▶ Working with the game-tree class
- ▶ Introducing Minimax
- ▶ Negamaxing
- ▶ AB Negamaxing
- ▶ Negascouting
- ▶ Implementing a tic-tac-toe rival
- ▶ Implementing a checkers rival

Introduction

In this chapter, you will learn about a family of algorithms for developing board game techniques to create artificial intelligence. They are based on the principle of a game tree (graph) that spans as we evaluate a state and decide to visit its neighbors. They also take into account board games for two rivals. But with a little bit of work, some of them can be extended to more players.

Working with the game-tree class

The game state can be represented in a lot of different ways, but you will learn how to create extendible classes in order to use the high-level board AI algorithms for different circumstances.

Getting ready...

It is important to be clear on object-oriented programming, specifically on inheritance and polymorphism. This is because we'll be creating generic functions that can be applied to a number of board game decisions and then writing specific subclasses that inherit and further specify these functions.

How to do it...

We will build two classes in order to represent game-tree with the help of the following steps:

1. Create the abstract class `Move`:

   ```
   using UnityEngine;
   using System.Collections;

   public abstract class Move
   {

   }
   ```

2. Create the pseudo-abstract class `Board`:

   ```
   using UnityEngine;
   using System.Collections;

   public class Board
   {
       protected int player;
       //next steps here
   }
   ```

3. Define the default constructor:

   ```
   public Board()
   {
       player = 1;
   }
   ```

4. Implement the virtual function for retrieving the next possible moves:

   ```
   public virtual Move[] GetMoves()
   {
       return new Move[0];
   }
   ```

5. Implement the virtual function for playing a move on the board:

```
public virtual Board MakeMove(Move m)
{
    return new Board();
}
```

6. Define the virtual function for testing whether the game is over:

```
public virtual bool IsGameOver()
{
    return true;
}
```

7. Implement the virtual function for retrieving the current player:

```
public virtual int GetCurrentPlayer()
{
    return player;
}
```

8. Implement the virtual function for testing the board's value for a given player:

```
public virtual float Evaluate(int player)
{
    return Mathf.NegativeInfinity;
}
```

9. Also, implement the virtual function for testing the board's value for the current player:

```
public virtual float Evaluate()
{
    return Mathf.NegativeInfinity;
}
```

How it works...

We have created the stepping stones for the next algorithms. The Board class works as a node in order to represent the current game state, and the Move class represents an edge. When the GetMoves function is called, we model the function for getting the edges in order to reach the neighbors of the current game state.

See also

For more theoretical insights about the techniques in this chapter, please refer to Russel and Norvig's *Artificial Intelligence: a Modern Approach* (adversarial search) and Ian Millington's *Artificial Intelligence for Games* (board games).

Introducing Minimax

Minimax is an algorithm based on the decision to minimize the possible loss for the worst case (maximum loss). Besides game development and game theory, Minimax is a decision rule and is also used in statistics, decision theory, and philosophy.

This technique was originally formulated for the two-player zero-sum game theory, meaning that one player's win is the opponent's loss. However, in this case, it is flexible enough to handle more than two players.

Getting ready...

It is important to know the difference between a dynamic member function and a static member function, as well as recursion. A dynamic member function is bound to the instance of the class, while the static member function is bound to the class itself. The static method allows us to call it without instantiating an object. This is great for general-purpose algorithms, such as the one developed in this recipe.

In the case of recursion, it's not always clear that (unlike iteration) this is an iterative process that requires a base case (also called the stop condition) and a recursive case (the one to keep iterating).

How to do it...

We will create the base class for handling all of our main algorithms and implement the `Minimax` function as follows:

1. Create the `BoardAI` class:

```
using UnityEngine;
using System.Collections;

public class BoardAI
{

}
```

2. Declare the `Minimax` function:

```
public static float Minimax(
        Board board,
        int player,
        int maxDepth,
        int currentDepth,
```

```
        ref Move bestMove)
{
    // next steps here
}
```

3. Consider the base case:

```
if (board.IsGameOver() || currentDepth == maxDepth)
    return board.Evaluate(player);
```

4. Set the initial values depending on the player:

```
bestMove = null;
float bestScore = Mathf.Infinity;
if (board.GetCurrentPlayer() == player)
    bestScore = Mathf.NegativeInfinity;
```

5. Loop through all the possible moves and return the best score:

```
foreach (Move m in board.GetMoves())
{
    // next steps here
}
return bestScore;
```

6. Create a new game state from the current move:

```
Board b = board.MakeMove(m);
float currentScore;
Move currentMove = null;
```

7. Start the recursion:

```
currentScore = Minimax(b, player, maxDepth, currentDepth + 1, ref
currentMove);
```

8. Validate the score for the current player:

```
if (board.GetCurrentPlayer() == player)
{
    if (currentScore > bestScore)
    {
        bestScore = currentScore;
        bestMove = currentMove;
    }
}
```

9. Validate the score for the adversary:

```
else
{
    if (currentScore < bestScore)
    {
        bestScore = currentScore;
        bestMove = currentMove;
    }
}
```

How it works...

The algorithm works as a bounded depth-first search. In each step, the move is chosen by selecting the option that maximizes the player's score and assuming the opponent will take the option for minimizing it, until a terminal (leaf) node is reached.

The move tracking is done using recursion, and the heuristic for selecting or assuming an option depends on the `Evaluate` function.

See also

> ▸ The *Working with the game-tree class* recipe in this chapter

Negamaxing

When we have a zero-sum game with only two players involved, we are able to improve Minimax, taking advantage of the principle that one player's loss is the other's gain. In this way, it is able to provide the same results as the Minimax algorithm. However, it does not track whose move it is.

Getting ready...

It is important to know the difference between a dynamic member function and a static member function, as well as recursion. A dynamic member function is bound to the instance of the class, while a static member function is bound to the class itself. The static method allows us to call it without instantiating an object. This is great for general-purpose algorithms, such as the one we are developing in this recipe.

In the case of recursion, it's not always clear that (unlike iteration) this is an iterative process that requires a base case (also called the stop condition) and a recursive case (the one to keep iterating).

How to do it...

We will add a new function to the `BoardAI` class as follows:

1. Create the `Negamax` function:

```
public static float Negamax(
        Board board,
        int maxDepth,
        int currentDepth,
        ref Move bestMove)
{
    // next steps here
}
```

2. Validate the base case:

```
if (board.IsGameOver() || currentDepth == maxDepth)
    return board.Evaluate();
```

3. Set the initial values:

```
bestMove = null;
float bestScore = Mathf.NegativeInfinity;
```

4. Loop through all the available moves and return the best score:

```
foreach (Move m in board.GetMoves())
{
    // next steps here
}
return bestScore;
```

5. Create a new game state from the current move:

```
Board b = board.MakeMove(m);
float recursedScore;
Move currentMove = null;
```

6. Start the recursion:

```
recursedScore = Negamax(b, maxDepth, currentDepth + 1, ref
currentMove);
```

7. Set the current score and update the best score and move, if necessary:

```
float currentScore = -recursedScore;
if (currentScore > bestScore)
{
    bestScore = currentScore;
    bestMove = m;
}
```

How it works...

The base algorithm works the same but, as we did before, there are some advantages. At each step in the recursion, the scores from the previous steps have their sign inverted. Instead of choosing the best option, the algorithm changes the sign of the score, eliminating the need to track whose move it is.

There's more...

As Negamax alternates the viewpoints between players at each step, the evaluate function used is the one with no parameters.

See also

- ► The *Working with the game-tree class* recipe
- ► The *Minimax* recipe

AB Negamaxing

There is still room for improving the Negamax algorithm. Despite its efficiency, the downside of the Negamax algorithm is that it examines more nodes than necessary (for example, board positions). To overcome this problem, we use Negamax with a search strategy called alpha-beta pruning.

Getting ready...

It is important to know the difference between a dynamic member function and a static member function, as well as recursion. A dynamic member function is bound to the instance of the class, while the static member function is bound to the class itself. The static method allows us to call it without instantiating an object. This is great for general-purpose algorithms, such as the one we are developing in this recipe.

In the case of recursion, it's not always clear that (unlike iteration) this is an iterative process that requires a base case (also called the stop condition) and a recursive case (the one to keep iterating).

How to do it...

We will add a new function to the `BoardAI` class as follows:

1. Create the `ABNegamax` function:

```
public static float ABNegamax(
        Board board,
        int player,
        int maxDepth,
        int currentDepth,
        ref Move bestMove,
        float alpha,
        float beta)
{
    // next steps here
}
```

2. Validate the base case:

```
if (board.IsGameOver() || currentDepth == maxDepth)
    return board.Evaluate(player);
```

3. Set the initial values:

```
bestMove = null;
float bestScore = Mathf.NegativeInfinity;
```

4. Loop through every available move and return the best score:

```
foreach (Move m in board.GetMoves())
{
    // next steps here
}
return bestScore;
```

5. Create a new game state from the current move:

```
Board b = board.MakeMove(m);
```

6. Set the values for calling the recursion:

```
float recursedScore;
Move currentMove = null;
int cd = currentDepth + 1;
float max = Mathf.Max(alpha, bestScore);
```

7. Start the recursion:

```
recursedScore = ABNegamax(b, player, maxDepth, cd, ref
currentMove, -beta, max);
```

8. Set the current score and update the best score and move if necessary. Also, stop the iteration if necessary:

```
float currentScore = -recursedScore;
if (currentScore > bestScore)
{
    bestScore = currentScore;
    bestMove = m;

    if (bestScore >= beta)
        return bestScore;
}
```

How it works...

Since we know the basic principle of the algorithm, let's concentrate on the search strategy. There are two values: alpha and beta. The alpha value is the lower score a player can achieve, thus avoiding considering any move where the opponent has the opportunity to lessen it. Similarly, the beta value is the upper limit; no matter how tempting the new option is, the algorithm assumes that the opponent won't give the opportunity to take it.

Given the alternation between each player (minimizing and maximizing), only one value needs to be checked at each step.

See also

▸ The *Working with the game-tree class* recipe
▸ The *Minimax* recipe
▸ The *Negamaxing* recipe

Negascouting

Including a search strategy also makes room for new challenges. Negascouting is the result of narrowing the search by improving the pruning heuristic. It is based on a concept called a **search window**, which is the interval between the alpha and beta values. So, reducing the search window increases the chance of a branch being pruned.

Getting ready...

It is important to know the difference between a dynamic member function and a static member function, as well as recursion. A dynamic member function is bound to the instance of the class, while the static member function is bound to the class itself. The static method allows us to call it without instantiating an object. This is great for general-purpose algorithms, such as the one we are developing in this recipe.

In the case of recursion, it's not always clear that (unlike iteration) this is an iterative process that requires a base case (also called the stop condition) and a recursive case (the one to keep iterating).

How to do it...

We will add a new function to the `BoardAI` class as follows:

1. Create the `ABNegascout` function:

```
public static float ABNegascout (
        Board board,
        int player,
        int maxDepth,
        int currentDepth,
        ref Move bestMove,
        float alpha,
        float beta)
{
    // next steps here
}
```

2. Validate the base case:

```
if (board.IsGameOver() || currentDepth == maxDepth)
    return board.Evaluate(player);
```

3. Set the initial values:

```
bestMove = null;
float bestScore = Mathf.NegativeInfinity;
float adaptiveBeta = beta;
```

4. Loop through every available move and return the best score:

```
foreach (Move m in board.GetMoves())
{
    // next steps here
}
return bestScore;
```

5. Create a new game state from the current move:

```
Board b = board.MakeMove(m);
```

6. Set the values for the recursion:

```
Move currentMove = null;
float recursedScore;
int depth = currentDepth + 1;
float max = Mathf.Max(alpha, bestScore);
```

7. Call the recursion:

```
recursedScore = ABNegamax(b, player, maxDepth, depth, ref
currentMove, -adaptiveBeta, max);
```

8. Set the current score and validate it:

```
float currentScore = -recursedScore;
if (currentScore > bestScore)
{
    // next steps here
}
```

9. Validate for pruning:

```
if (adaptiveBeta == beta || currentDepth >= maxDepth - 2)
{
    bestScore = currentScore;
    bestMove = currentMove;
}
```

10. Otherwise, take a look around:

```
else
{
    float negativeBest;
    negativeBest = ABNegascout(b, player, maxDepth, depth, ref
bestMove, -beta, -currentScore);
    bestScore = -negativeBest;
}
```

11. Stop the loop if necessary. Otherwise, update the adaptive value:

```
if (bestScore >= beta)
    return bestScore;

adaptiveBeta = Mathf.Max(alpha, bestScore) + 1f;
```

How it works...

This algorithm works by examining the first move of each node. The following moves are examined using a scout pass with a narrower window based on the first move. If the pass fails, it is repeated using a full-width window. As a result, a large number of branches are pruned and failures are avoided.

See also

► The *AB Negamaxing* recipe

Implementing a tic-tac-toe rival

In order to make use of the previous recipes, we will devise a way to implement a rival for a popular game: tic-tac-toe. Not only does it help us extend the base classes, but it also gives us a way to create rivals for our own board games.

Getting ready...

We will need to create a specific move class for the tic-tac-toe board derived from the parent class we created at the beginning of the chapter:

```
using UnityEngine;
using System.Collections;

public class MoveTicTac : Move
{
    public int x;
    public int y;
    public int player;

    public MoveTicTac(int x, int y, int player)
    {
        this.x = x;
        this.y = y;
        this.player = player;
    }
}
```

How to do it...

We will create a new class, deriving it from `Board`, override its parent's methods, and create new ones.

1. Create the `BoardTicTac` class, deriving it from `Board`, and add the corresponding member variables for storing the board's values:

```
using UnityEngine;
using System;
using System.Collections;
using System.Collections.Generic;

public class BoardTicTac : Board
{
    protected int[,] board;
    protected const int ROWS = 3;
    protected const int COLS = 3;
}
```

2. Implement the default constructor:

```
public BoardTicTac(int player = 1)
{
    this.player = player;
    board = new int[ROWS, COLS];
    board[1,1] = 1;
}
```

3. Define the function for retrieving the next player in turn:

```
private int GetNextPlayer(int p)
{
    if (p == 1)
        return 2;
    return 1;
}
```

4. Create a function for evaluating a given position regarding a given player:

```
private float EvaluatePosition(int x, int y, int p)
{
    if (board[y, x] == 0)
        return 1f;
    else if (board[y, x] == p)
        return 2f;
    return -1f;
}
```

5. Define a function for evaluating the neighbors of a given position regarding a given player:

```
private float EvaluateNeighbours(int x, int y, int p)
{
    float eval = 0f;
    int i, j;
    for (i = y - 1; i < y + 2; y++)
    {
        if (i < 0 || i >= ROWS)
            continue;
        for (j = x - 1; j < x + 2; j++)
        {
            if (j < 0 || j >= COLS)
                continue;
            if (i == j)
                continue;
            eval += EvaluatePosition(j, i, p);
        }
    }
    return eval;
}
```

6. Implement a constructor for building new states with values:

```
public BoardTicTac(int[,] board, int player)
{
    this.board = board;
    this.player = player;
}
```

7. Override the member function for getting the available moves from the current state:

```
public override Move[] GetMoves()
{
    List<Move> moves = new List<Move>();
    int i;
    int j;
    for (i = 0; i < ROWS; i++)
    {
        for (j = 0; j < COLS; j++)
        {
            if (board[i, j] != 0)
                continue;
            MoveTicTac m = new MoveTicTac(j, i, player);
            moves.Add(m);
        }
```

```
        }
        return moves.ToArray();
    }
```

8. Override the function for retrieving a new state from a given move:

```
public override Board MakeMove(Move m)
{
    MoveTicTac move = (MoveTicTac)m;
    int nextPlayer = GetNextPlayer(move.player);
    int[,] copy = new int[ROWS, COLS];
    Array.Copy(board, 0, copy, 0, board.Length);
    copy[move.y, move.x] = move.player;
    BoardTicTac b = new BoardTicTac(copy, nextPlayer);
    return b;
}
```

9. Define the function for evaluating the current state, given a player:

```
public override float Evaluate(int player)
{
    float eval = 0f;
    int i, j;
    for (i = 0; i < ROWS; i++)
    {
        for (j = 0; j < COLS; j++)
        {
            eval += EvaluatePosition(j, i, player);
            eval += EvaluateNeighbours(j, i, player);
        }
    }
    return eval;
}
```

10. Implement the function for evaluating the current state of the current player:

```
public override float Evaluate()
{
    float eval = 0f;
    int i, j;
    for (i = 0; i < ROWS; i++)
    {
        for (j = 0; j < COLS; j++)
        {
            eval += EvaluatePosition(j, i, player);
```

```
                eval += EvaluateNeighbours(j, i, player);
            }
        }
        return eval;
    }
```

How it works...

We define a new type of move for the board that works well with the base algorithms because they make use of it only at a high level as a data structure. The recipe's bread and butter come from overriding the virtual functions from the `Board` class in order to model the problem. We use a two-dimensional integer array for storing the players' moves on the board (0 represents an empty place), and we work out a heuristic for defining the value of a given state regarding its neighbors.

There is more...

The functions for evaluating a board's (state) score have an admissible heuristic, but it's probably not optimal. It is up to us to revisit this problem and refactor the body of the aforementioned functions in order to have a better tuned rival.

See also

▸   The *Working with the game-tree class* recipe

Implementing a checkers rival

You will learn how to extend the previous recipes with an advanced example. In this case, you will learn how to model a checkers (draughts) board and its pieces in order to comply with the necessary functions to be used with our board-AI framework.

This approach uses a chess board (8 x 8) and its respective number of pieces (12). However, it can be easily parameterized in order to change these values in case we want to have a differently sized board.

Getting ready...

First, we need to create a new type of movement for this particular case called
`MoveDraughts`:

```
using UnityEngine;
using System.Collections;

public class MoveDraughts : Move
{
    public PieceDraughts piece;
    public int x;
    public int y;
    public bool success;
    public int removeX;
    public int removeY;
}
```

This data structure stores the piece to be moved, the new x and y coordinates if the
movement is a successful capture, and the position of the piece to be removed.

How to do it...

We will implement two core classes for modeling the pieces and the board, respectively.
This is a long process, so read each step carefully:

1. Create a new file called `PieceDraughts.cs` and add the following statements:

   ```
   using UnityEngine;
   using System.Collections;
   using System.Collections.Generic;
   ```

2. Add the `PieceColor` data type:

   ```
   public enum PieceColor
   {
       WHITE,
       BLACK
   };
   ```

3. Add the `PieceType` data enum:

   ```
   public enum PieceType
   {
       MAN,
       KING
   };
   ```

4. Start building the `PieceDraughts` class:

```
public class PieceDraughts : MonoBehaviour
{
    public int x;
    public int y;
    public PieceColor color;
    public PieceType type;
    // next steps here
}
```

5. Define the function for setting up the piece logically:

```
public void Setup(int x, int y,
        PieceColor color,
        PieceType type = PieceType.MAN)
{
    this.x = x;
    this.y = y;
    this.color = color;
    this.type = type;
}
```

6. Define the function for moving the piece on the board:

```
public void Move (MoveDraughts move, ref PieceDraughts [,] board)
{
    board[move.y, move.x] = this;
    board[y, x] = null;
    x = move.x;
    y = move.y;
    // next steps here
}
```

7. If the move is a capture, remove the corresponding piece:

```
if (move.success)
{
    Destroy(board[move.removeY, move.removeX]);
    board[move.removeY, move.removeX] = null;
}
```

8. Stop the process if the piece is `King`:

```
if (type == PieceType.KING)
    return;
```

9. Change the type of piece if it is `Man` and it reaches the opposite border:

```
int rows = board.GetLength(0);
if (color == PieceColor.WHITE && y == rows)
    type = PieceType.KING;
if (color == PieceColor.BLACK && y == 0)
    type = PieceType.KING;
```

10. Define the function for checking if a move is inside the bounds of the board:

```
private bool IsMoveInBounds(int x, int y, ref PieceDraughts[,]
board)
{
    int rows = board.GetLength(0);
    int cols = board.GetLength(1);
    if (x < 0 || x >= cols || y < 0 || y >= rows)
        return false;
    return true;
}
```

11. Define the general function for retrieving the possible moves:

```
public Move[] GetMoves(ref PieceDraughts[,] board)
{
    List<Move> moves = new List<Move>();
    if (type == PieceType.KING)
        moves = GetMovesKing(ref board);
    else
        moves = GetMovesMan(ref board);
    return moves.ToArray();
}
```

12. Start implementing the function for retrieving the moves when the piece's type is `Man`:

```
private List<Move> GetMovesMan(ref PieceDraughts[,] board)
{
    // next steps here
}
```

13. Add the variable for storing the two possible moves:

```
List<Move> moves = new List<Move>(2);
```

14. Define the variable for holding the two possible horizontal options:

```
int[] moveX = new int[] { -1, 1 };
```

15. Define the variable for holding the vertical direction depending on the piece's color:

```
int moveY = 1;
if (color == PieceColor.BLACK)
    moveY = -1;
```

16. Implement the loop for iterating through the two possible options and return the available moves. We will implement the body of the loop in the next step:

```
foreach (int mX in moveX)
{
    // next steps
}
return moves;
```

17. Declare two new variable for computing the next position to be considered:

```
int nextX = x + mX;
int nextY = y + moveY;
```

18. Test the possible option if the move is out of bounds:

```
if (!IsMoveInBounds(nextX, y, ref board))
    continue;
```

19. Continue with the next option if the move is being blocked by a piece of the same color:

```
PieceDraughts p = board[moveY, nextX];
if (p != null && p.color == color)
    continue;
```

20. Create a new move to be added to the list because we're good-to-go:

```
MoveDraughts m = new MoveDraughts();
m.piece = this;
```

21. Create a simple move if the position is available:

```
if (p == null)
{
    m.x = nextX;
    m.y = nextY;
}
```

22. Otherwise, test whether the piece can be captured and modify the move accordingly:

```
else
{
    int hopX = nextX + mX;
    int hopY = nextY + moveY;
    if (!IsMoveInBounds(hopX, hopY, ref board))
```

```
            continue;
      if (board[hopY, hopX] != null)
            continue;
      m.y = hopX;
      m.x = hopY;
      m.success = true;
      m.removeX = nextX;
      m.removeY = nextY;
}
```

23. Add the move to the list:

    ```
    moves.Add(m);
    ```

24. Start to implement the function for retrieving the available moves when the piece's type is `King`:

    ```
    private List<Move> GetMovesKing(ref PieceDraughts[,] board)
    {
        // next steps here
    }
    ```

25. Declare the variable for holding the possible moves:

    ```
    List<Move> moves = new List<Move>();
    ```

26. Create the variables for searching in four directions:

    ```
    int[] moveX = new int[] { -1, 1 };
    int[] moveY = new int[] { -1, 1 };
    ```

27. Start implementing the loop for checking all the possible moves, and retrieve those moves. The next step will implement the body of the inner loop:

    ```
    foreach (int mY in moveY)
    {
        foreach (int mX in moveX)
        {
            // next steps here
        }
    }
    return moves;
    ```

28. Create the variables for testing the moves and advances:

    ```
    int nowX = x + mX;
    int nowY = y + mY;
    ```

29. Create a loop for going in that direction until the board's bounds are reached:

```
while (IsMoveInBounds(nowX, nowY, ref board))
{
    // next steps here
}
```

30. Get the position's piece reference:

```
PieceDraughts p = board[nowY, nowX];
```

31. If it is a piece of the same color, go no further:

```
if (p != null && p.color == color)
    break;
```

32. Define a variable for creating the new available move:

```
MoveDraughts m = new MoveDraughts();
m.piece = this;
```

33. Create a simple move if the position is available:

```
if (p == null)
{
    m.x = nowX;
    m.y = nowY;
}
```

34. Otherwise, test whether the piece can be captured and modify the move accordingly:

```
else
{
    int hopX = nowX + mX;
    int hopY = nowY + mY;
    if (!IsMoveInBounds(hopX, hopY, ref board))
        break;
    m.success = true;
    m.x = hopX;
    m.y = hopY;
    m.removeX = nowX;
    m.removeY = nowY;
}
```

35. Add the move and advance a step towards the current direction:

```
moves.Add(m);
nowX += mX;
nowY += mY;
```

36. Create a new class called `BoardDraughts` in a new file:

```
using UnityEngine;
using System.Collections;
using System.Collections.Generic;

public class BoardDraughts : Board
{
    public int size = 8;
    public int numPieces = 12;
    public GameObject prefab;
    protected PieceDraughts[,] board;
}
```

37. Implement the `Awake` function:

```
void Awake()
{
    board = new PieceDraughts[size, size];
}
```

38. Start implementing the `Start` function. It is important to note that this may vary depending on your game's spatial representation:

```
void Start()
{
    // TODO
    // initialization and board set up
    // your implementation may vary

    // next steps here
}
```

39. Throw an error message if the template object doesn't have an attached `PieceDraught` script:

```
PieceDraughts pd = prefab.GetComponent<PieceDraughts>();
if (pd == null)
{
    Debug.LogError("No PieceDraught component detected");
    return;
}
```

40. Add iterator variables:

```
int i;
int j;
```

41. Implement the loop for placing the white pieces:

```
int piecesLeft = numPieces;
for (i = 0; i < size; i++)
{
    if (piecesLeft == 0)
        break;
    int init = 0;
    if (i % 2 != 0)
        init = 1;
    for (j = init; j < size; j+=2)
    {
        if (piecesLeft == 0)
            break;
        PlacePiece(j, i);
        piecesLeft--;
    }
}
```

42. Implement the loop for placing the black pieces:

```
piecesLeft = numPieces;
for (i = size - 1; i >= 0; i--)
{
    if (piecesLeft == 0)
        break;
    int init = 0;
    if (i % 2 != 0)
        init = 1;
    for (j = init; j < size; j+=2)
    {
        if (piecesLeft == 0)
            break;
        PlacePiece(j, i);
        piecesLeft--;
    }
}
```

43. Implement the function for placing a specific piece. This could change in your game depending on its visualization:

```
private void PlacePiece(int x, int y)
{
    // TODO
    // your own transformations
    // according to space placements
    Vector3 pos = new Vector3();
```

```
    pos.x = (float)x;
    pos.y = -(float)y;
    GameObject go = GameObject.Instantiate(prefab);
    go.transform.position = pos;
    PieceDraughts p = go.GetComponent<PieceDraughts>();
    p.Setup(x, y, color);
    board[y, x] = p;
}
```

44. Implement the `Evaluate` function with no parameters:

```
public override float Evaluate()
{
    PieceColor color = PieceColor.WHITE;
    if (player == 1)
        color = PieceColor.BLACK;
    return Evaluate(color);
}
```

45. Implement the `Evaluate` function with a parameter:

```
public override float Evaluate(int player)
{
    PieceColor color = PieceColor.WHITE;
    if (player == 1)
        color = PieceColor.BLACK;
    return Evaluate(color);
}
```

46. Start implementing the general function for evaluation:

```
private float Evaluate(PieceColor color)
{
    // next steps here
}
```

47. Define the variables for holding the evaluation and assigning points:

```
float eval = 1f;
float pointSimple = 1f;
float pointSuccess = 5f;
```

48. Create variables for holding the board's bounds:

```
int rows = board.GetLength(0);
int cols = board.GetLength(1);
```

49. Define variables for iteration:

```
int i;
int j;
```

50. Iterate throughout the board to look for moves and possible captures:

```
for (i = 0; i < rows; i++)
{
    for (j = 0; j < cols; j++)
    {
        PieceDraughts p = board[i, j];
        if (p == null)
            continue;
        if (p.color != color)
            continue;
        Move[] moves = p.GetMoves(ref board);
        foreach (Move mv in moves)
        {
            MoveDraughts m = (MoveDraughts)mv;
            if (m.success)
                eval += pointSuccess;
            else
                eval += pointSimple;
        }
    }
}
```

51. Retrieve the evaluation value:

```
return eval;
```

52. Start developing the function for retrieving the board's available moves:

```
public override Move[] GetMoves()
{
    // next steps here
}
```

53. Define the variables for holding the moves and the board's boundaries, and handling iteration:

```
List<Move> moves = new List<Move>();
int rows = board.GetLength(0);
int cols = board.GetLength(1);
int i;
int j;
```

54. Get the moves from all the available pieces on the board:

```
for (i = 0; i < rows; i++)
{
    for (j = 0; i < cols; j++)
    {
```

```
            PieceDraughts p = board[i, j];
            if (p == null)
                continue;
            moves.AddRange(p.GetMoves(ref board));
        }
    }
```

55. Return the moves found:

```
    return moves.ToArray();
```

How it works...

The board works in a similar fashion to the previous board, but it has a more complex process due to the rules of the game. The movements are tied to the pieces' moves, thus creating a cascading effect that must be handled carefully. Each piece has two types of movement, depending on its color and type.

As we can see, the high-level rules are the same. It just requires a little bit of patience and thinking in order to develop good evaluation functions and procedures for retrieving the board's available moves.

There is more...

The Evaluate function is far from being perfect. We implemented a heuristic based solely on the number of available moves and captured opponent pieces, giving room for improvement in order to avoid movements where a player's piece could be captured in the rival's next move.

Also, we should make our own changes to the PlacePiece function in the BoardDraughts class. We implemented a direct method that probably doesn't fit your game's spatial setup.

7
Learning Techniques

In this chapter, we will explore the world of machine learning through the following topics:

- ▸ Predicting actions with an N-Gram predictor
- ▸ Improving the predictor: Hierarchical N-Gram
- ▸ Learning to use a Naïve Bayes classifier
- ▸ Learning to use decision trees
- ▸ Learning to use reinforcement
- ▸ Learning to use artificial neural networks

.Introduction

In this chapter, we will explore the field of machine learning. This is a very extensive and intrinsic field in which even AAA titles have a hard time due to the amount of time that the techniques require for fine-tuning and experimentation.

However, the recipes that are contained in this chapter will give us a great head start in our endeavor to learn and apply machine-learning techniques to our games. They are used in several different ways, but the one we usually appreciate the most is difficulty adjustment.

Finally, you are advised to complement the recipes with the reading of more formal books on the subject, in order to gain theoretical insights that lie beyond the scope of this chapter.

Predicting actions with an N-Gram predictor

Predicting actions is a great way to give players a challenge by going from random selection to selection based on past actions. One way to implement learning is by using probabilities in order to predict what the player will do next, and that's what an N-Gram predictor does.

To predict the next choice, N-Gram predictors hold a record of the probabilities of making a decision (which is usually a move), given all combinations of choices for the previous *n* moves.

Getting ready...

This recipe makes use of general types. It is recommended that we have at least a basic understanding of how they work because it's critical that we use them well.

The first thing to do is implement a data type for holding the actions and their probabilities; we'll call it `KeyDataRecord`.

The `KeyDataReconrd.cs` file should look like this:

```
using System.Collections;
using System.Collections.Generic;

public class KeyDataRecord<T>
{
    public Dictionary<T, int> counts;
    public int total;

    public KeyDataRecord()
    {
        counts = new Dictionary<T, int>();
    }
}
```

How to do it...

Building N-Gram predictor is divided into five big steps. They are as follows:

1. Create the general class within a file named exactly the same:
   ```
   using System.Collections;
   using System.Collections.Generic;
   using System.Text;

   public class NGramPredictor<T>
   {
   ```

```
        private int nValue;
        private Dictionary<string, KeyDataRecord<T>> data;
    }
```

2. Implement the constructor for initializing the member variables:

```
public NGramPredictor(int windowSize)
{
    nValue = windowSize + 1;
    data = new Dictionary<string, KeyDataRecord<T>>();
}
```

3. Implement a static function for converting a set of actions into a string key:

```
public static string ArrToStrKey(ref T[] actions)
{
    StringBuilder builder = new StringBuilder();
    foreach (T a in actions)
    {
        builder.Append(a.ToString());
    }
    return builder.ToString();
}
```

4. Define the function for registering a set of sequences:

```
public void RegisterSequence(T[] actions)
{
    string key = ArrToStrKey(ref actions);
    T val = actions[nValue - 1];
    if (!data.ContainsKey(key))
        data[key] = new KeyDataRecord<T>();
    KeyDataRecord<T> kdr = data[key];
    if (kdr.counts.ContainsKey(val))
        kdr.counts[val] = 0;
    kdr.counts[val]++;
    kdr.total++;
}
```

5. Finally, implement the function for computing the prediction of the best action to take:

```
public T GetMostLikely(T[] actions)
{
    string key = ArrToStrKey(ref actions);
    KeyDataRecord<T> kdr = data[key];
    int highestVal = 0;
    T bestAction = default(T);
    foreach (KeyValuePair<T,int> kvp in kdr.counts)
```

```
        {
            if (kvp.Value > highestVal)
            {
                bestAction = kvp.Key;
                highestVal = kvp.Value;
            }
        }
        return bestAction;
    }
```

How it works...

The predictor registers a set of actions according to the size of the window (the number of actions to register in order to make predictions) and assigns them a resulting value. For example, having a window size of 3, the first three are saved as a key to predict that it's possible that the fourth one may follow.

The prediction function computes how likely it is for an action to be the one that follows, given a set of previous actions. The more registered actions, the more accurate the predictor will be (with some limitations).

There is more...

It is important to consider that the object of type T must override both the `ToString` function and Equals function in an admissible way for it to work correctly as an index in the internal dictionaries.

Improving the predictor: Hierarchical N-Gram

The N-Gram predictor can be improved by having a handler with several other predictors ranging from 1 to n, and obtaining the best possible action after comparing the best guess from each one of them.

Getting ready...

We need to make some adjustments prior to implementing the hierarchical N-Gram predictor.

Add the following member function to the `NGramPredictor` class:

```
public int GetActionsNum(ref T[] actions)
{
    string key = ArrToStrKey(ref actions);
```

```
    if (!data.ContainsKey(key))
        return 0;
    return data[key].total;
}
```

How to do it...

Just like the N-Gram predictor, building the hierarchical version takes a few steps:

1. Create the new class:

```
using System;
using System.Collections;
using System.Text;

public class HierarchicalNGramP<T>
{

    public int threshold;
    public NGramPredictor<T>[] predictors;
    private int nValue;
}
```

2. Implement the constructor for initializing member values:

```
public HierarchicalNGramP(int windowSize)
{
    nValue = windowSize + 1;
    predictors = new NGramPredictor<T>[nValue];
    int i;
    for (i = 0; i < nValue; i++)
        predictors[i] = new NGramPredictor<T>(i + 1);
}
```

3. Define a function for registering a sequence, just like its predecessor:

```
public void RegisterSequence(T[] actions)
{
    int i;
    for (i = 0; i < nValue; i++)
    {
        T[] subactions = new T[i+1];
        Array.Copy(actions, nValue - i - 1, subactions, 0, i+1);
        predictors[i].RegisterSequence(subactions);
    }
}
```

4. Finally, implement the function for computing the prediction:

```
public T GetMostLikely(T[] actions)
{
    int i;
    T bestAction = default(T);
    for (i = 0; i < nValue; i++)
    {
        NGramPredictor<T> p;
        p = predictors[nValue - i - 1];
        T[] subactions = new T[i + 1];
        Array.Copy(actions, nValue - i - 1, subactions, 0, i + 1);
        int numActions = p.GetActionsNum(ref actions);
        if (numActions > threshold)
            bestAction = p.GetMostLikely(actions);
    }
    return bestAction;
}
```

How it works...

The hierarchical N-Gram predictor works almost exactly like its predecessor, with the difference being that it holds a set of predictors and computes each main function using its children. Registering sequences, or finding out the most likely future action, works by decomposing the set of actions and feeding the children with them.

Learning to use Naïve Bayes classifiers

Learning to use examples could be hard even for humans. For example, given a list of examples for two sets of values, it's not always easy to see the connection between them. One way of solving this problem would be to classify one set of values and then give it a try, and that's where classifier algorithms come in handy.

Naïve Bayes classifiers are prediction algorithms for assigning labels to problem instances; they apply probability and Bayes' theorem with a strong-independence assumption between the variables to analyze. One of the key advantages of Bayes' classifiers is scalability.

Getting ready...

Since it is hard to build a general classifier, we will build ours assuming that the inputs are positive- and negative-labeled examples. So, the first thing that we need to address is defining the labels that our classifier will handle using an `enum` data structure called NBCLabel:

```
public enum NBCLabel
{
    POSITIVE,
    NEGATIVE
}
```

How to do it...

The classifier we'll build only takes five great steps:

1. Create the class and its member variables:

```
using UnityEngine;
using System.Collections;
using System.Collections.Generic;

public class NaiveBayesClassifier : MonoBehaviour
{
    public int numAttributes;
    public int numExamplesPositive;
    public int numExamplesNegative;

    public List<bool> attrCountPositive;
    public List<bool> attrCountNegative;
}
```

2. Define the `Awake` method for initialization:

```
void Awake()
{
    attrCountPositive = new List<bool>();
    attrCountNegative = new List<bool>();
}
```

3. Implement the function for updating the classifier:

```
public void UpdateClassifier(bool[] attributes, NBCLabel label)
{
    if (label == NBCLabel.POSITIVE)
    {
        numExamplesPositive++;
```

```
            attrCountPositive.AddRange(attributes);
        }
        else
        {
            numExamplesNegative++;
            attrCountNegative.AddRange(attributes);
        }
    }
```

4. Define the function for computing the Naïve probability:

```
public float NaiveProbabilities(
        ref bool[] attributes,
        bool[] counts,
        float m,
        float n)
{
    float prior = m / (m + n);
    float p = 1f;
    int i = 0;
    for (i = 0; i < numAttributes; i++)
    {
        p /= m;
        if (attributes[i] == true)
            p *= counts[i].GetHashCode();
        else
            p *= m - counts[i].GetHashCode();
    }
    return prior * p;
}
```

5. Finally, implement the function for prediction:

```
public bool Predict(bool[] attributes)
{
    float nep = numExamplesPositive;
    float nen = numExamplesNegative;
    float x = NaiveProbabilities(ref attributes,
attrCountPositive.ToArray(), nep, nen);
    float y = NaiveProbabilities(ref attributes,
attrCountNegative.ToArray(), nen, nep);
    if (x >= y)
        return true;
    return false;
}
```

How it works...

The `UpdateClassifier` function takes the example input values and stores them. This is the first function to be called. The `NaiveProbabilities` function is the one responsible for computing the probabilities for the prediction function to work. Finally, the `Predict` function is the second one to be called by us in order to get the results of classification.

Learning to use decision trees

We already learned the power and flexibility of decision trees for adding a decision-making component to our game. Furthermore, we can also build them dynamically through supervised learning. That's why we're revisiting them in this chapter.

There are several algorithms for building decision trees that are suited for different uses such as prediction and classification. In our case, we'll explore decision-tree learning by implementing the ID3 algorithm.

Getting ready...

Despite having built decision trees in a previous chapter, and the fact that they're based on the same principles as the ones that we will implement now, we will use different data types for our implementation needs in spite of the learning algorithm.

We will need two data types: one for the decision nodes and one for storing the examples to be learned.

The code for the `DecisionNode` data type is as follows:

```
using System.Collections.Generic;

public class DecisionNode
{
    public string testValue;
    public Dictionary<float, DecisionNode> children;

    public DecisionNode(string testValue = "")
    {
        this.testValue = testValue;
        children = new Dictionary<float, DecisionNode>();
    }
}
```

The code for the `Example` data type is as follows:

```
using UnityEngine;
using System.Collections.Generic;

public enum ID3Action
{
    STOP, WALK, RUN
}

public class ID3Example : MonoBehaviour
{
    public ID3Action action;
    public Dictionary<string, float> values;

    public float GetValue(string attribute)
    {
        return values[attribute];
    }
}
```

How to do it...

We will create the `ID3` class with several functions for computing the resulting decision tree.

1. Create the `ID3` class:

```
using UnityEngine;
using System.Collections.Generic;
public class ID3 : MonoBehaviour
{
    // next steps
}
```

2. Start the implementation of the function responsible for splitting the attributes into sets:

```
public Dictionary<float, List<ID3Example>> SplitByAttribute(
        ID3Example[] examples,
        string attribute)
{
    Dictionary<float, List<ID3Example>> sets;
    sets = new Dictionary<float, List<ID3Example>>();
    // next step
}
```

3. Iterate though all the examples received, and extract their value in order to assign them to a set:

```
foreach (ID3Example e in examples)
{
    float key = e.GetValue(attribute);
    if (!sets.ContainsKey(key))
        sets.Add(key, new List<ID3Example>());
    sets[key].Add(e);
}
return sets;
```

4. Create the function for computing the entropy for a set of examples:

```
public float GetEntropy(ID3Example[] examples)
{
    if (examples.Length == 0) return 0f;
    int numExamples = examples.Length;
    Dictionary<ID3Action, int> actionTallies;
    actionTallies = new Dictionary<ID3Action, int>();
    // next steps
}
```

5. Iterate through all of the examples to compute their action quota:

```
foreach (ID3Example e in examples)
{
    if (!actionTallies.ContainsKey(e.action))
        actionTallies.Add(e.action, 0);
    actionTallies[e.action]++;
}
```

6. Compute the entropy :

```
int actionCount = actionTallies.Keys.Count;
if (actionCount == 0) return 0f;
float entropy = 0f;
float proportion = 0f;
foreach (int tally in actionTallies.Values)
{
    proportion = tally / (float)numExamples;
    entropy -= proportion * Mathf.Log(proportion, 2);
}
return entropy;
```

7. Implement the function for computing the entropy for all the sets of examples. This is very similar to the preceding one; in fact, it uses it:

```
public float GetEntropy(
        Dictionary<float, List<ID3Example>> sets,
        int numExamples)
{
    float entropy = 0f;
    foreach (List<ID3Example> s in sets.Values)
    {
        float proportion;
        proportion = s.Count / (float)numExamples;
        entropy -= proportion * GetEntropy(s.ToArray());
    }
    return entropy;
}
```

8. Define the function for building a decision tree:

```
public void MakeTree(
        ID3Example[] examples,
        List<string> attributes,
        DecisionNode node)
{
    float initEntropy = GetEntropy(examples);
    if (initEntropy <= 0) return;
    // next steps
}
```

9. Declare and initialize all the required members for the task:

```
int numExamples = examples.Length;
float bestInfoGain = 0f;
string bestSplitAttribute = "";
float infoGain = 0f;
float overallEntropy = 0f;
Dictionary<float, List<ID3Example>> bestSets;
bestSets = new Dictionary<float, List<ID3Example>>();
Dictionary<float, List<ID3Example>> sets;
```

10. Iterate through all the attributes in order to get the best set based on the information gain:

```
foreach (string a in attributes)
{
    sets = SplitByAttribute(examples, a);
    overallEntropy = GetEntropy(sets, numExamples);
    infoGain = initEntropy - overallEntropy;
```

```
        if (infoGain > bestInfoGain)
        {
            bestInfoGain = infoGain;
            bestSplitAttribute = a;
            bestSets = sets;
        }
    }
```

11. Select the root node based on the best split attribute, and rearrange the remaining attributes for building the rest of the tree:

```
node.testValue = bestSplitAttribute;
List<string> newAttributes = new List<string>(attributes);
newAttributes.Remove(bestSplitAttribute);
```

12. Iterate through all the remaining attributes. calling the function recursively:

```
foreach (List<ID3Example> set in bestSets.Values)
{
    float val = set[0].GetValue(bestSplitAttribute);
    DecisionNode child = new DecisionNode();
    node.children.Add(val, child);
    MakeTree(set.ToArray(), newAttributes, child);
}
```

How it works...

The class is modular in terms of functionality. It doesn't store any information but is able to compute and retrieve everything needed for the function that builds the decision tree. SplitByAttribute takes the examples and divides them into sets that are needed for computing their entropy. ComputeEntropy is an overloaded function that computes a list of examples and all the sets of examples using the formulae defined in the ID3 algorithm. Finally, MakeTree works recursively in order to build the decision tree, getting hold of the most significant attribute.

See also

▶ *Chapter 3, Decision Making*, the *Choosing through a decision tree* recipe

Learning to use reinforcement

Imagine that we need to come up with an enemy that needs to select different actions over time as the player progresses through the game and his or her patterns change, or a game for training different types of pets that have free will to some extent.

For these types of tasks, we can use a series of techniques aimed at modeling learning based on experience. One of these algorithms is Q-learning, which will be implemented in this recipe.

Getting ready...

Before delving into the main algorithm, it is necessary to have certain data structures implemented. We need to define a structure for game state, another for game actions, and a class for defining an instance of the problem. They can coexist in the same file.

The following is an example of the data structure for defining a game state:

```
public struct GameState
{
    // TODO
    // your state definition here
}
```

Next is an example of the data structure for defining a game action:

```
public struct GameAction
{
    // TODO
    // your action definition here
}
```

Finally, we will build the data type for defining a problem instance:

1. Create the file and class:

   ```
   public class ReinforcementProblem
   {
   }
   ```

2. Define a virtual function for retrieving a random state. Depending on the type of game we're developing, we are interested in random states considering the current state of the game:

   ```
   public virtual GameState GetRandomState()
   {
       // TODO
       // Define your own behaviour
       return new GameState();
   }
   ```

3. Define a virtual function for retrieving all the available actions from a given game state:

```
public virtual GameAction[] GetAvailableActions(GameState s)
{
    // TODO
    // Define your own behaviour
    return new GameAction[0];
}
```

4. Define a virtual function for carrying out an action, and then retrieving the resulting state and reward:

```
public virtual GameState TakeAction(
        GameState s,
        GameAction a,
        ref float reward)
{
    // TODO
    // Define your own behaviour
    reward = 0f;
    return new GameState();
}
```

How to do it...

We will implement two classes. The first one stores values in a dictionary for learning purposes, and the second one is the class that actually holds the Q-learning algorithm:

1. Create the QValueStore class:

```
using UnityEngine;
using System.Collections.Generic;

public class QValueStore : MonoBehaviour
{
    private Dictionary<GameState, Dictionary<GameAction, float>>
store;
}
```

2. Implement the constructor:

```
public QValueStore()
{
    store = new Dictionary<GameState, Dictionary<GameAction,
float>>();
}
```

3. Define the function for getting the resulting value of taking an action in a game state. Carefully craft this, considering an action cannot be taken in that particular state:

```
public virtual float GetQValue(GameState s, GameAction a)
{
    // TODO: your behaviour here
    return 0f;
}
```

4. Implement the function for retrieving the best action to take in a certain state:

```
public virtual GameAction GetBestAction(GameState s)
{
    // TODO: your behaviour here
    return new GameAction();
}
```

5. Implement the function for :

```
public void StoreQValue(
        GameState s,
        GameAction a,
        float val)
{
    if (!store.ContainsKey(s))
    {
        Dictionary<GameAction, float> d;
        d = new Dictionary<GameAction, float>();
        store.Add(s, d);
    }
    if (!store[s].ContainsKey(a))
    {
        store[s].Add(a, 0f);
    }
    store[s][a] = val;
}
```

6. Let's move on to the QLearning class, which will run the algorithm:

```
using UnityEngine;
using System.Collections;

public class QLearning : MonoBehaviour
{
    public QValueStore store;
}
```

7. Define the function for retrieving random actions from a given set:

```
private GameAction GetRandomAction(GameAction[] actions)
{
    int n = actions.Length;
    return actions[Random.Range(0, n)];
}
```

8. Implement the learning function. Be advised that this is split into several steps. Start by defining it. Take into consideration that this is a coroutine:

```
public IEnumerator Learn(
        ReinforcementProblem problem,
        int numIterations,
        float alpha,
        float gamma,
        float rho,
        float nu)
{
    // next steps
}
```

9. Validate that the store list is initialized:

```
if (store == null)
    yield break;
```

10. Get a random state:

```
GameState state = problem.GetRandomState();
for (int i = 0; i < numIterations; i++)
{
    // next steps
}
```

11. Return null for the current frame to keep running:

```
yield return null;
```

12. Validate against the length of the walk :

```
if (Random.value < nu)
    state = problem.GetRandomState();
```

13. Get the available actions from the current game state:

```
GameAction[] actions;
actions = problem.GetAvailableActions(state);
GameAction action;
```

14. Get an action depending on the value of the randomness of exploration:

```
if (Random.value < rho)
    action = GetRandomAction(actions);
else
    action = store.GetBestAction(state);
```

15. Calculate the new state for taking the selected action on the current state and the resulting reward value:

```
float reward = 0f;
GameState newState;
newState = problem.TakeAction(state, action, ref reward);
```

16. Get the q value, given the current game, and take action and the best action for the new state computed before:

```
float q = store.GetQValue(state, action);
GameAction bestAction = store.GetBestAction(newState);
float maxQ = store.GetQValue(newState, bestAction);
```

17. Apply the Q-learning formula:

```
q = (1f - alpha) * q + alpha * (reward + gamma * maxQ);
```

18. Store the computed q value, giving its parents as indices:

```
store.StoreQValue(state, action, q);
state = newState;
```

How it works...

In the Q-learning algorithm, the game world is treated as a state machine. It is important to take note of the meaning of the parameters:

- alpha: This is the learning rate
- gamma: This is the discount rate
- rho: This is the randomness of exploration
- nu: This is the length of the walk

Learning to use artificial neural networks

Imagine a way to make an enemy or game system emulate the way the brain works. That's how neural networks operate. They are based on a neuron, we call it Perceptron, and the sum of several neurons; its inputs and outputs are what makes a neural network.

In this recipe, we will learn how to build a neural system, starting from Perceptron, all the way to joining them in order to create a network.

Getting ready...

We will need a data type for handling raw input; this is called `InputPerceptron`:

```
public class InputPerceptron
{
    public float input;
    public float weight;
}
```

How to do it...

We will implement two big classes. The first one is the implementation for the `Perceptron` data type, and the second one is the data type handling the neural network:

1. Implement a `Perceptron` class derived from the `InputPerceptron` class that was previously defined:

```
public class Perceptron : InputPerceptron
{
    public InputPerceptron[] inputList;
    public delegate float Threshold(float x);
    public Threshold threshold;
    public float state;
    public float error;
}
```

2. Implement the constructor for setting the number of inputs:

```
public Perceptron(int inputSize)
{
    inputList = new InputPerceptron[inputSize];
}
```

3. Define the function for processing the inputs:

```
public void FeedForward()
{
    float sum = 0f;
    foreach (InputPerceptron i in inputList)
    {
        sum += i.input * i.weight;
    }
    state = threshold(sum);
}
```

4. Implement the functions for adjusting weights:

```
public void AdjustWeights(float currentError)
{
    int i;
    for (i = 0; i < inputList.Length; i++)
    {
        float deltaWeight;
        deltaWeight = currentError * inputList[i].weight * state;
        inputList[i].weight = deltaWeight;
        error = currentError;
    }
}
```

5. Define a function for funneling the weights with regard to the type of input:

```
public float GetIncomingWeight()
{
    foreach (InputPerceptron i in inputList)
    {
        if (i.GetType() == typeof(Perceptron))
            return i.weight;
    }
    return 0f;
}
```

6. Create the class for handling the set of Perceptron as a network:

```
using UnityEngine;
using System.Collections;

public class MLPNetwork : MonoBehaviour
{
    public Perceptron[] inputPer;
    public Perceptron[] hiddenPer;
    public Perceptron[] outputPer;
}
```

7. Implement the function for transmitting inputs from one end to the other of the neural network:

```
public void GenerateOutput(Perceptron[] inputs)
{
    int i;
    for (i = 0; i < inputs.Length; i++)
        inputPer[i].state = inputs[i].input;

    for (i = 0; i < hiddenPer.Length; i++)
```

```
            hiddenPer[i].FeedForward();

        for (i = 0; i < outputPer.Length; i++)
            outputPer[i].FeedForward();
    }
```

8. Define the function for propelling the computation that actually emulates learning:

```
public void BackProp(Perceptron[] outputs)
{
    // next steps
}
```

9. Traverse the output layer for computing values:

```
int i;
for (i = 0; i < outputPer.Length; i++)
{
    Perceptron p = outputPer[i];
    float state = p.state;
    float error = state * (1f - state);
    error *= outputs[i].state - state;
    p.AdjustWeights(error);
}
```

10. Traverse the internal `Perceptron` layers, but the input layer:

```
for (i = 0; i < hiddenPer.Length; i++)
{
    Perceptron p = outputPer[i];
    float state = p.state;
    float sum = 0f;
    for (i = 0; i < outputs.Length; i++)
    {
        float incomingW = outputs[i].GetIncomingWeight();
        sum += incomingW * outputs[i].error;
        float error = state * (1f - state) * sum;
        p.AdjustWeights(error);
    }
}
```

11. Implement a high-level function for ease of use:

```
public void Learn(
        Perceptron[] inputs,
        Perceptron[] outputs)
{
    GenerateOutput(inputs);
    BackProp(outputs);
}
```

How it works...

We implemented two types of Perceptrons in order to define the ones that handle external input and the ones internally connected to each other. That's why the *basic* Perceptron class derives from the latter category. The `FeedForward` function handles the inputs and irrigates them along the network. Finally, the function for back propagation is the one responsible for adjusting the weights. This *weight adjustment* is the emulation of learning.

Creating emergent particles using a harmony search

Being a musician myself, this recipe is one that is close to my heart. Imagine a group of musicians with a base theme in mind. But, they've never played with each other, and as the song changes, they must adapt to the core tones with their instruments and their styles. The emulation of this adaptation is implemented using an algorithm called harmony search.

Getting ready...

We will need to define an objective function as a delegate in order to set it up before calling the function.

How to do it...

We will now implement the algorithm in a class:

1. Create the `HarmonySearch` class:

   ```
   using UnityEngine;
   using System.Collections;

   public class HarmonySearch : MonoBehaviour
   {

   }
   ```

2. Define the public inputs that are to be tuned:

   ```
   [Range(1, 100)]
   public int memorySize = 30;
   public int pitchNum;
   // consolidation rate
   [Range(0.1f, 0.99f)]
   public float consRate = 0.9f;
   ```

```
// adjustment rate
[Range(0.1f, 0.99f)]
public float adjsRate = 0.7f;
public float range = 0.05f;
public int numIterations;
[Range(0.1f, 1.0f)]
public float par = 0.3f;
```

3. Define a list of bounds. This is a `Vector2`, so x will represent the lowest bound and y the highest bound. The number of bounds must be equal to the number of pitches:

```
public Vector2[] bounds;
```

4. Define the private members for the algorithm:

```
private float[,] memory;
private float[] solution;
private float fitness;
private float best;
```

5. Implement the initialization function:

```
private void Init()
{
    memory = new float[memorySize, pitchNum];
    solution = new float[memorySize];
    fitness = ObjectiveFunction(memory);
}
```

6. Start defining the function for creating harmony:

```
private float[] CreateHarmony()
{
    float[] vector = new float[pitchNum];
    int i;
    // next steps
}
```

7. Iterate through the number of pitches (instruments):

```
for (i = 0; i < pitchNum; i++)
{
    // next steps
}
```

8. Compute the new number of the possible new harmonies, given a random value:

```
if (Random.value < consRate)
{
    int r = Random.Range(0, memory.Length);
    float val = memory[r, i];
```

```
        if (Random.value < adjsRate)
            val = val + range * Random.Range(-1f, 1f);
        if (val < bounds[i].x)
            val = bounds[i].x;
        if (val > bounds[i].y)
            val = bounds[i].y;
        vector[i] = val;
    }
```

9. Define the value in case it needs to be randomized:

```
else
{
    vector[i] = Random.Range(bounds[i].x, bounds[i].y);
}
```

10. Retrieve the new vector:

```
return vector;
```

11. Define the function that will make everything work:

```
public float[] Run()
{
    // next steps
}
```

12. Initialize the values:

```
Init();
int iterations = numIterations;
float best = Mathf.Infinity;
```

13. Call the previous functions and computations to find the best list of pitches:

```
while (iterations != 0)
{
    iterations--;
    float[] harm = CreateHarmony();
    fitness = ObjectiveFunction(harm);
    best = Mathf.Min(fitness, best);
    memory = harm;
}
```

14. Return the best list of pitches:

```
return
```

How it works...

The algorithm initializes all the values, given the public inputs and its inner members. It iterates several times in order to find the best list of pitches among the set of bounds and the different tones created using the previously defined objective function.

8
Miscellaneous

In this chapter, you will learn different techniques for:

- ▸ Handling random numbers better
- ▸ Building an air-hockey rival
- ▸ Devising a table-football competitor
- ▸ Creating a tennis rival
- ▸ Creating mazes procedurally
- ▸ Implementing a self-driving car
- ▸ Managing race difficulty using a rubber-banding system

Introduction

In this final chapter, we will introduce new techniques, and use algorithms that we have learned in the previous chapters in order to create new behaviors that don't quite fix in a definite category. This is a chapter to have fun and get another glimpse of how to mix different techniques in order to achieve different goals.

Handling random numbers better

Sometimes, we need to create random behaviors that don't differ too much from a pivot point; this is the case of an aiming behavior. A normalized random behavior will shoot equally along the x and the y axes over a given distance from the aiming point. However, we would like most of the bullets to aim closer to the target because that's the expected behavior.

Most of the random functions out there return normalized values along the range given to them, and those are the expected results. Nonetheless, this is not completely useful for certain features in game development, as we just said. We will implement a random function to be used in our games with normal distribution instead of a normal distribution.

Getting ready

It is important to understand the differences between uniform and normal distribution. In the following figure, we can see a graphical representation of the behavior we're looking for by applying normal distribution with the example mentioned in the introductory text.

In the figure on the left-hand side, the uniform distribution spreads through the whole circle, and it is intended to be used in general random distributions. However, while developing other techniques, such as gun aiming, the desired random distribution will look more like the image on the right-hand side.

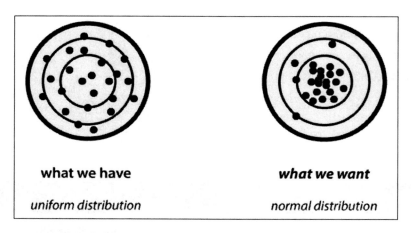

what we have

uniform distribution

what we want

normal distribution

How to do it...

We will build a simple class as follows:

1. Create the RandomGaussian class:

```
using UnityEngine;

public class RandomGaussian
{
    // next steps
}
```

2. Define the `RangeAdditive` member function that initializes the necessary member variables:

```
public static float RangeAdditive(params Vector2[] values)
{
    float sum = 0f;
    int i;
    float min, max;
    // next steps
}
```

3. Check whether the number of parameters equals zero. If so, create three new values:

```
if (values.Length == 0)
{
    values = new Vector2[3];
    for (i = 0; i < values.Length; i++)
        values[i] = new Vector2(0f, 1f);
}
```

4. Sum all the values:

```
for (i = 0; i < values.Length; i++)
{
    min = values[i].x;
    max = values[i].y;
    sum += Random.Range(min, max);
}
```

5. Return the resulting random number:

```
return sum;
```

There's more...

We should always strive for efficiency. That's why there's another way of delivering a similar result. In this case, we could implement a new member function based on the solution offered by Rabin and others (refer to the proceeding *See also* section):

```
public static ulong seed = 61829450;
public static float Range()
{
    double sum = 0;
    for (int i = 0; i < 3; i++)
    {
        ulong holdseed = seed;
        seed ^= seed << 13;
```

```
        seed ^= seed >> 17;
        seed ^= seed << 5;
        long r = (long)(holdseed * seed);
        sum += r * (1.0 / 0x7FFFFFFFFFFFFFFF);
    }
    return (float)sum;
}
```

See also

▶ For further information on the theory behind the Gaussian random generator and other advanced generators, please refer to the book *Game AI Pro* by Steve Rabin, article number 3

Building an air-hockey rival

Air hockey is probably one of the most popular games enjoyed by players of all ages during the golden age of arcades, and they are still found everywhere. With the advent of touchscreen mobile devices, developing an air-hockey game is a fun way to not only test physics engines, but also to develop intelligent rivals despite the apparently low complexity of the game.

Getting ready

This is a technique based on some of the algorithms that we learned in *Chapter 1, Movement*, such as `Seek`, `Arrive`, and `Leave`, and the ray casting knowledge that is employed in several other recipes, such as path smoothing.

It is necessary for the paddle game object to be used by the agent to have the `AgentBehaviour`, `Seek`, and `Leave` components attached, as it is used by the current algorithm. Also, it is important to tag the objects used as walls, that is, the ones containing the box colliders, as seen in the following figure:

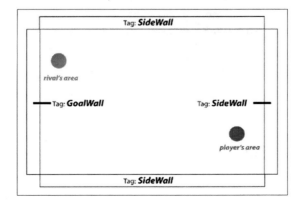

Finally, it is important to create an `enum` type for handling the rival's state:

```
public enum AHRState
{
    ATTACK,
    DEFEND,
    IDLE
}
```

How to do it...

This is a long class, so it is important to carefully follow these steps:

1. Create the rival's class:

   ```
   using UnityEngine;
   using System.Collections;

   public class AirHockeyRival : MonoBehaviour
   {
       // next steps
   }
   ```

2. Declare the public variables for setting it up and fine-tuning it:

   ```
   public GameObject puck;
   public GameObject paddle;
   public string goalWallTag = "GoalWall";
   public string sideWallTag = "SideWall";
   [Range(1, 10)]
   public int maxHits;
   ```

3. Declare the private variables:

   ```
   float puckWidth;
   Renderer puckMesh;
   Rigidbody puckBody;
   AgentBehaviour agent;
   Seek seek;
   Leave leave;
   AHRState state;
   bool hasAttacked;
   ```

4. Implement the `Awake` member function for setting up private classes, given the public ones:

   ```
   public void Awake()
   {
   ```

```
        puckMesh = puck.GetComponent<Renderer>();
        puckBody = puck.GetComponent<Rigidbody>();
        agent = paddle.GetComponent<AgentBehaviour>();
        seek = paddle.GetComponent<Seek>();
        leave = paddle.GetComponent<Leave>();
        puckWidth = puckMesh.bounds.extents.z;
        state = AHRState.IDLE;
        hasAttacked = false;
        if (seek.target == null)
            seek.target = new GameObject();
        if (leave.target == null)
            leave.target = new GameObject();
}
```

5. Declare the `Update` member function. The following steps will define its body:

```
public void Update()
{
    // next steps
}
```

6. Check the current state and call the proper functions:

```
switch (state)
{
    case AHRState.ATTACK:
        Attack();
        break;
    default:
    case AHRState.IDLE:
        agent.enabled = false;
        break;
    case AHRState.DEFEND:
        Defend();
        break;
}
```

7. Call the function for resetting the active state for hitting the puck:

```
AttackReset();
```

8. Implement the function for setting up the state from external objects:

```
public void SetState(AHRState newState)
{
    state = newState;
}
```

9. Implement the function for retrieving the distance from paddle to puck:

```
private float DistanceToPuck()
{
    Vector3 puckPos = puck.transform.position;
    Vector3 paddlePos = paddle.transform.position;
    return Vector3.Distance(puckPos, paddlePos);
}
```

10. Declare the member function for attacking. The following steps will define its body:

```
private void Attack()
{
    if (hasAttacked)
        return;
    // next steps
}
```

11. Enable the agent component and calculate the distance to puck:

```
agent.enabled = true;
float dist = DistanceToPuck();
```

12. Check whether the puck is out of reach. If so, just follow it:

```
if (dist > leave.dangerRadius)
{
    Vector3 newPos = puck.transform.position;
    newPos.z = paddle.transform.position.z;
    seek.target.transform.position = newPos;
    seek.enabled = true;
    return;
}
```

13. Attack the puck if it is within reach:

```
hasAttacked = true;
seek.enabled = false;
Vector3 paddlePos = paddle.transform.position;
Vector3 puckPos = puck.transform.position;
Vector3 runPos = paddlePos - puckPos;
runPos = runPos.normalized * 0.1f;
runPos += paddle.transform.position;
leave.target.transform.position = runPos;
leave.enabled = true;
```

14. Implement the function for resetting the parameter for hitting the puck:

```
private void AttackReset()
{
    float dist = DistanceToPuck();
    if (hasAttacked && dist < leave.dangerRadius)
        return;
    hasAttacked = false;
    leave.enabled = false;
}
```

15. Define the function for defending the goal:

```
private void Defend()
{
    agent.enabled = true;
    seek.enabled = true;
    leave.enabled = false;
    Vector3 puckPos = puckBody.position;
    Vector3 puckVel = puckBody.velocity;
    Vector3 targetPos = Predict(puckPos, puckVel, 0);
    seek.target.transform.position = targetPos;
}
```

16. Implement the function for predicting the puck's position in the future:

```
private Vector3 Predict(Vector3 position, Vector3 velocity, int
numHit)
{
    if (numHit == maxHits)
        return position;
    // next steps
}
```

17. Cast a ray, given the position and the direction of the puck:

```
RaycastHit[] hits = Physics.RaycastAll(position, velocity.
normalized);
RaycastHit hit;
```

18. Check the hit results:

```
foreach (RaycastHit h in hits)
{
    string tag = h.collider.tag;
    // next steps
}
```

19. Check whether it collides with the goal wall. Base case:

```
if (tag.Equals(goalWallTag))
{
    position = h.point;
    position += (h.normal * puckWidth);
    return position;
}
```

20. Check whether it collides with a side wall. Recursive case:

```
if (tag.Equals(sideWallTag))
{
    hit = h;
    position = hit.point + (hit.normal * puckWidth);
    Vector3 u = hit.normal;
    u *= Vector3.Dot(velocity, hit.normal);
    Vector3 w = velocity - u;
    velocity = w - u;
    break;
}
// end of foreach
```

21. Enter the recursive case. This is done from the `foreach` loop:

```
return Predict(position, velocity, numHit + 1);
```

How it works...

The agent calculates the puck's next hits given its current velocity until the calculation results in the puck hitting the agent's wall. This calculation gives a point for the agent to move its paddle toward it. Furthermore, it changes to the attack mode when the puck is close to its paddle and is moving towards it. Otherwise, it changes to idle or defend depending on the new distance.

See also

▶ Chapter 1, *Movement* recipes *Pursuing and evading* and *Arriving and leaving* recipes

Devising a table-football competitor

Another common table game that has made its way into the digital realm is table football. In this recipe, we will create a competitor, imitating the way a human plays the game and using some techniques that emulate human senses and limitations.

Getting ready

In this recipe, we will use the knowledge gained from *Chapter 5*, *Agent Awareness*, and the emulation of vision.

First, it is important to have a couple of `enum` data structures, as shown in the following code:

```
public enum TFRAxisCompare
{
    X, Y, Z
}

public enum TFRState
{
    ATTACK, DEFEND, OPEN
}
```

How to do it...

This is a very extensive recipe. We'll build a couple of classes, one for the table-football bar and the other for the main AI agent that handles the bars, as follows:

1. Create a class for the bar that will be handled by the AI:

```
using UnityEngine;
using System.Collections;

public class TFRBar : MonoBehaviour
{
    [HideInInspector]
    public int barId;
    public float barSpeed;
    public float attackDegrees = 30f;
    public float defendDegrees = 0f;
    public float openDegrees = 90f;
    public GameObject ball;
    private Coroutine crTransition;
    private bool isLocked;
    // next steps
}
```

2. Implement the `Awake` function:

```
void Awake()
{
    crTransition = null;
    isLocked = false;
}
```

3. Define the function for setting the state of the bar:

```
public void SetState(TFRState state, float speed = 0f)
{
    // next steps
}
```

4. Check whether it is locked (after beginning a movement). This is optional:

```
// optional
if (isLocked)
    return;
isLocked = true;
```

5. Validate the speed:

```
if (speed == 0)
    speed = barSpeed;
float degrees = 0f;
```

6. Validate the state and make a decision out of it:

```
switch(state)
{
    case TFRState.ATTACK:
        degrees = attackDegrees;
        break;
    default:
    case TFRState.DEFEND:
        degrees = defendDegrees;
        break;
    case TFRState.OPEN:
        degrees = openDegrees;
        break;
}
```

7. Execute the transition:

```
if (crTransition != null)
    StopCoroutine(crTransition);
crTransition = StartCoroutine(Rotate(degrees, speed));
```

8. Define the function for rotating the bar:

```
public IEnumerator Rotate(float target, float speed)
{
    // next steps
}
```

9. Implement the internal body for the transition:

```
while (transform.rotation.x != target)
{
    Quaternion rot = transform.rotation;
    if (Mathf.Approximately(rot.x, target))
    {
        rot.x = target;
        transform.rotation = rot;
    }
    float vel = target - rot.x;
    rot.x += speed * Time.deltaTime * vel;
    yield return null;
}
```

10. Restore the bar to its default position:

```
isLocked = false;
transform.rotation = Quaternion.identity;
```

11. Implement the function for moving the bar from side to side:

```
public void Slide(float target, float speed)
{
    Vector3 targetPos = transform.position;
    targetPos.x = target;
    Vector3 trans = transform.position - targetPos;
    trans *= speed * Time.deltaTime;
    transform.Translate(trans, Space.World);
}
```

12. Create the class for the main AI:

```
using UnityEngine;
using System.Collections;
using System.Collections.Generic;

public class TFRival : MonoBehaviour
{

    public string tagPiece = "TFPiece";
    public string tagWall = "TFWall";
    public int numBarsToHandle = 2;
    public float handleSpeed;
    public float attackDistance;
    public TFRAxisCompare depthAxis = TFRAxisCompare.Z;
    public TFRAxisCompare widthAxis = TFRAxisCompare.X;
    public GameObject ball;
```

```
        public GameObject[] bars;
        List<GameObject>[] pieceList;
        // next
    }
```

13. Implement the `Awake` function for initializing the piece list:

```
    void Awake()
    {
        int numBars = bars.Length;
        pieceList = new List<GameObject>[numBars];
        for (int i = 0; i < numBars; i++)
        {
            pieceList[i] = new List<GameObject>();
        }
    }
```

14. Start implementing the `Update` function:

```
    void Update()
    {
        int[] currBars = GetNearestBars();
        Vector3 ballPos = ball.transform.position;
        Vector3 barsPos;
        int i;
        // next steps
    }
```

15. Define the status for each bar, depending on the ball's position:

```
    for (i = 0; i < currBars.Length; i++)
    {
        GameObject barObj = bars[currBars[i]];
        TFRBar bar = barObj.GetComponent<TFRBar>();
        barsPos = barObj.transform.position;
        float ballVisible = Vector3.Dot(barsPos, ballPos);
        float dist = Vector3.Distance(barsPos, ballPos);
        if (ballVisible > 0f && dist <= attackDistance)
            bar.SetState(TFRState.ATTACK, handleSpeed);
        else if (ballVisible > 0f)
            bar.SetState(TFRState.DEFEND);
        else
            bar.SetState(TFRState.OPEN);
    }
```

16. Implement the `OnGUI` function. This will handle the prediction at 30 frames per second:

```
public void OnGUI()
{
    Predict();
}
```

17. Define the prediction function with its member values:

```
private void Predict()
{
    Rigidbody rb = ball.GetComponent<Rigidbody>();
    Vector3 position = rb.position;
    Vector3 velocity = rb.velocity.normalized;
    int[] barsToCheck = GetNearestBars();
    List<GameObject> barsChecked;
    GameObject piece;
    barsChecked = new List<GameObject>();
    int id = -1;
    // next steps
}
```

18. Define the main loop for checking the ball's trajectory:

```
do
{
    RaycastHit[] hits = Physics.RaycastAll(position, velocity.
normalized);
    RaycastHit wallHit = null;
    foreach (RaycastHit h in hits)
    {
        // next steps
    }

} while (barsChecked.Count == numBarsToHandle);
```

19. Get the object of the collision and check whether it is a bar and whether it has been checked already:

```
GameObject obj = h.collider.gameObject;
if (obj.CompareTag(tagWall))
    wallHit = h;
if (!IsBar(obj))
    continue;
if (barsChecked.Contains(obj))
    continue;
```

20. Check, if it is a bar, whether it is among those closest to the ball:

```
bool isToCheck = false;
for (int i = 0; i < barsToCheck.Length; i++)
{
    id = barsToCheck[i];
    GameObject barObj = bars[id];
    if (obj == barObj)
    {
        isToCheck = true;
        break;
    }
}
if (!isToCheck)
    continue;
```

21. Get the bar collision point and calculate the movement for blocking the ball with the closest piece:

```
Vector3 p = h.point;
piece = GetNearestPiece(h.point, id);
Vector3 piecePos = piece.transform.position;
float diff = Vector3.Distance(h.point, piecePos);
obj.GetComponent<TFRBar>().Slide(diff, handleSpeed);
barsChecked.Add(obj);
```

22. Otherwise, recalculate with the wall's hitting point:

```
c
```

23. Create the function for setting the pieces to the proper bar:

```
void SetPieces()
{
    // next steps
}
```

24. Create a dictionary for comparing the pieces' depth:

```
// Create a dictionary between z-index and bar
Dictionary<float, int> zBarDict;
zBarDict = new Dictionary<float, int>();
int i;
```

25. Set up the dictionary:

```
for (i = 0; i < bars.Length; i++)
{
    Vector3 p = bars[i].transform.position;
```

```
        float index = GetVectorAxis(p, this.depthAxis);
        zBarDict.Add(index, i);
    }
```

26. Start mapping the pieces to the bars:

```
// Map the pieces to the bars
GameObject[] objs = GameObject.FindGameObjectsWithTag(tagPiece);
Dictionary<float, List<GameObject>> dict;
dict = new Dictionary<float, List<GameObject>>();
```

27. Assign pieces to their proper dictionary entry:

```
foreach (GameObject p in objs)
{
    float zIndex = p.transform.position.z;
    if (!dict.ContainsKey(zIndex))
        dict.Add(zIndex, new List<GameObject>());
    dict[zIndex].Add(p);
}
```

28. Define the function for getting a bar's index, given a position:

```
int GetBarIndex(Vector3 position, TFRAxisCompare axis)
{
    // next steps
}
```

29. Validate it:

```
int index = 0;
if (bars.Length == 0)
    return index;
```

30. Declare the necessary member values:

```
float pos = GetVectorAxis(position, axis);
float min = Mathf.Infinity;
float barPos;
Vector3 p;
```

31. Traverse the list of bars:

```
for (int i = 0; i < bars.Length; i++)
{
    p = bars[i].transform.position;
    barPos = GetVectorAxis(p, axis);
    float diff = Mathf.Abs(pos - barPos);
    if (diff < min)
    {
```

```
        min = diff;
        index = i;
    }
}
```

32. Retrieve the found index:

```
return index;
```

33. Implement the function for calculating the vector axis:

```
float GetVectorAxis(Vector3 v, TFRAxisCompare a)
{
    if (a == TFRAxisCompare.X)
        return v.x;
    if (a == TFRAxisCompare.Y)
        return v.y;
    return v.z;
}
```

34. Define the function for getting the nearest bars to the ball:

```
public int[] GetNearestBars()
{
    // next steps
}
```

35. Initialize all the necessary member variables:

```
int numBars = Mathf.Clamp(numBarsToHandle, 0, bars.Length);
Dictionary<float, int> distBar;
distBar = new Dictionary<float, int>(bars.Length);
List<float> distances = new List<float>(bars.Length);
int i;
Vector3 ballPos = ball.transform.position;
Vector3 barPos;
```

36. Traverse the bars:

```
for (i = 0; i < bars.Length; i++)
{
    barPos = bars[i].transform.position;
    float d = Vector3.Distance(ballPos, barPos);
    distBar.Add(d, i);
    distances.Add(d);
}
```

37. Sort the distances:

```
distances.Sort();
```

38. Get the distances and use the dictionary in an inverse way:

```
int[] barsNear = new int[numBars];
for (i = 0; i < numBars; i++)
{
    float d = distances[i];
    int id = distBar[d];
    barsNear[i] = id;
}
```

39. Retrieve the bar IDs:

```
return barsNear;
```

40. Implement the function for checking whether a given object is a bar:

```
private bool IsBar(GameObject gobj)
{
    foreach (GameObject b in bars)
    {
        if (b == gobj)
            return true;
    }
    return false;
}
```

41. Start implementing the function for retrieving the closest piece of a bar, given a position:

```
private GameObject GetNearestPiece(Vector3 position, int barId)
{
    // next steps
}
```

42. Define the necessary member variables:

```
float minDist = Mathf.Infinity;
float dist;
GameObject piece = null;
```

43. Traverse the list of pieces and calculate the closest one:

```
foreach (GameObject p in pieceList[barId])
{
    dist = Vector3.Distance(position, p.transform.position);
    if (dist < minDist)
    {
        minDist = dist;
        piece = p;
    }
}
```

44. Retrieve the piece:

```
return piece;
```

How it works...

The table-football competitor draws on the skills developed from the air-hockey rival. This means casting rays to get the trajectory of the ball and moving the nearest bar considering the pieces. It also moves the bar, depending on whether the rival is attacking or defending, so that it can block the ball or let it go further.

See also

▶   The *Seeing using a collider-based system* recipe in *Chapter 5, Agent Awareness*

Creating mazes procedurally

This is a completely new recipe oriented toward having fun while creating maps and levels procedurally. The main recipe works by creating a maze completely procedurally. Furthermore, we will explore a gray area, where both level design and procedurally generated content meet.

Getting ready

In this recipe, it is important to understand the concepts of Binary Space Partitioning and the Breadth-first Search algorithm learned in *Chapter 2, Navigation*.

How to do it...

We will implement two classes, one for the nodes to be partitioned and one for holding all the nodes and the maze representation, as follows:

1. Create the BSPNode class and its members:

```
using UnityEngine;

[System.Serializable]
public class BSPNode
{
    public Rect rect;
    public BSPNode nodeA;
    public BSPNode nodeB;
}
```

2. Implement the class constructor:

```
public BSPNode(Rect rect)
{
    this.rect = rect;
    nodeA = null;
    nodeB = null;
}
```

3. Define the function for splitting the node into two subregions:

```
public void Split(float stopArea)
{
    // next steps
}
```

4. Validate its base case:

```
if (rect.width * rect.height >= stopArea)
    return;
```

5. Initialize all the necessary function variables:

```
bool vertSplit = Random.Range(0, 1) == 1;
float x, y, w, h;
Rect rectA, rectB;
```

6. Compute the horizontal split:

```
if (!vertSplit)
{
    x = rect.x;
    y = rect.y;
    w = rect.width;
    h = rect.height / 2f;
    rectA = new Rect(x, y, w, h);
    y += h;
    rectB = new Rect(x, y, w, h);
}
```

7. Compute the vertical split:

```
else
{
    x = rect.x;
    y = rect.y;
    w = rect.width / 2f;
    h = rect.height;
```

```
        rectA = new Rect(x, y, w, h);
        x += w;
        rectB = new Rect(x, y, w, h);
    }
```

8. Create the class for handling the dungeon and declare all its member variables:

```
using UnityEngine;
using System.Collections.Generic;

public class Dungeon : MonoBehaviour
{
    public Vector2 dungeonSize;
    public float roomAreaToStop;
    public float middleThreshold;
    public GameObject floorPrefab;

    private BSPNode root;
    private List<BSPNode> nodeList;
}
```

9. Implement the function for splitting:

```
public void Split()
{
    float x, y, w, h;
    x = dungeonSize.x / 2f * -1f;
    y = dungeonSize.y / 2f * -1f;
    w = dungeonSize.x;
    h = dungeonSize.y;
    Rect rootRect = new Rect(x, y, w, h);
    root = new BSPNode(rootRect);
}
```

10. Implement the function for drawing the maze using the nodes:

```
public void DrawNode(BSPNode n)
{
    GameObject go = Instantiate(floorPrefab) as GameObject;
    Vector3 position = new Vector3(n.rect.x, 0f, n.rect.y);
    Vector3 scale = new Vector3(n.rect.width, 1f, n.rect.height);
    go.transform.position = position;
    go.transform.localScale = scale;
}
```

How it works...

We divided the maze into two big data structures. The logical side that is handled via the BSP nodes and the visual and construction representation handled by the main `Maze` class. The idea behind this representation is to divide the space twice as many times as necessary until a condition is met. This is the Binary Space Partitioning.

We then created rooms for the leave nodes, and finally, we connected the regions on the tree from the bottom to the top (leaves to root).

There's more...

- There's another technique that is a little bit simpler, but it requires more input from the art or level-design team. It creates a level with BFS using random pieces in a list and connects them.
- The pieces can be rotated.
- It can be improved by using the random function learned previously and tuning the pieces' placement on the list.

See also

- The *Finding the shortest path in a grid with BFS* recipe in *Chapter 2, Navigation*

Implementing a self-driving car

What fun is a racing game without competitors? This is one of the most difficult subjects in artificial intelligence for games. It is usually tackled by creating *cheater* agents that disable certain limitations that are always imposed on the player, such as physics behaviors; this is because these limitations can create erratic or imprecise behaviors when evaluated by AI. In our case, we will approach the problem organically using techniques from a previous chapter.

Getting ready

In this chapter, we will explore how to create an autonomous car using advanced techniques from *Chapter 1, Movement*, such as following a path and avoiding walls. So, it is important to have grasped the knowledge behind them.

How to do it...

1. Create an empty **GameObject**.
2. Attach the **Agent** component.
3. Attach the **FollowPath** component.
4. Attach the **WallAvoid** component.
5. Create the track using the track pieces with the **PathNode** component.
6. Tag the track borders as walls.
7. Make sure the track is complete.

How it works...

By working with the system from the previous chapters, we can easily create a simple, yet flexible, system to create intelligent cars.

See also

▶ The *Following a path* and *Avoiding walls* recipes in *Chapter 1, Movement*

Managing race difficulty using a rubber-banding system

We usually want to create experiences that adapt to the player, and racing games are a good field for this, given that there is this gap of the cheater agent.

In this case, we will explore a middle ground for this using a framework that allows you to come up with your own heuristic for managing the speed of the vehicle given its status. It doesn't matter if it is an arcade racing game or simulation; the framework aims to work in a similar fashion for both the cases.

Getting ready

It is important to have grasped the basic skills in *Chapter 1, Movement*, in order to be able to develop a strategy to extend the framework for your own needs—that is, understanding the principles of how the agent class works and how the behaviors help the player move toward an object. In a nutshell, we are talking about vector operations.

How to do it...

We will implement three different classes for handling low-level and high-level AIs as follows:

1. Create the class for the basic rival agent:

```
using UnityEngine;

public class RacingRival : MonoBehaviour
{
    public float distanceThreshold;
    public float maxSpeed;
    public Vector3 randomPos;
    protected Vector3 targetPosition;
    protected float currentSpeed;
    protected RacingCenter ghost;
}
```

2. Implement the `Start` function:

```
void Start()
{
    ghost = FindObjectOfType<RacingCenter>();
}
```

3. Define the `Update` function for handling the target position to follow:

```
public virtual void Update()
{
    targetPosition = transform.position + randomPos;
    AdjustSpeed(targetPosition);
}
```

4. Define your function for adjusting the speed accordingly:

```
public virtual void AdjustSpeed(Vector3 targetPosition)
{
    // TODO
    // your own behaviour here
}
```

5. Create the class for handling the ghost rider or an invincible racer:

```
using UnityEngine;

public class RacingCenter : RacingRival
{
    public GameObject player;
}
```

6. Implement the initial function for finding its target:

```
void Start()
{
    player = GameObject.FindGameObjectWithTag("Player");
}
```

7. Override the Update function, so the invincible car can adapt to the player's behavior:

```
public override void Update()
{
    Vector3 playerPos = player.transform.position;
    float dist = Vector3.Distance(transform.position,
    playerPos);
    if (dist > distanceThreshold)
    {
        targetPosition = player.transform.position;
        base.Update();
    }
}
```

8. Implement its special behavior:

```
public override void AdjustSpeed(Vector3 targetPosition)
{

    // TODO
    // Use in case the base behaviour also applies
    base.AdjustSpeed(targetPosition);
}
```

9. Create the class for handling the high-level AI:

```
using UnityEngine;

public class Rubberband : MonoBehaviour
{
    RacingCenter ghost;
    RacingRival[] rivals;
}
```

10. Assign each racer its random position in the rubber system. We are using a circular rubber band in this case:

```
void Start()
{
    ghost = FindObjectOfType<RacingCenter>();
    rivals = FindObjectsOfType<RacingRival>();
```

```
      foreach (RacingRival r in rivals)
      {
           if (ReferenceEquals(r, ghost))
               continue;
           r.randomPos = Random.insideUnitSphere;
           r.randomPos.y = ghost.transform.position.y;
      }
 }
```

How it works...

The high-level AI rubber system assigns the positions to be held by the racers. Each racer has its own behavior for adjusting speed, especially the invincible racer. This agent works as the center of the mass of the rubber band. If its dance from the player exceeds the threshold, it will adapt. Otherwise, it'll stay just the same, wobbling.

Index

A

A*
extending, for coordination 121-124
A* algorithm
improving, for memory 82-85
used, for finding best promising path 79-82
AB Negamaxing 186-188
actions
predicting, with N-Gram predictor 208-210
agents
avoiding 22-24
air-hockey rival
building 236-241
A*mbush algorithm 121-124
arriving 9, 10
artificial neural networks
using 224-228
awareness
creating, in stealth game 169-176

B

behaviors
blending, by priority 28-30
blending, by weight 26, 27
combining, steering pipeline used 30-33
template, creating 2-6
behavior trees
implementing 102-104
Breadth-First Search (BFS) algorithm
used, for finding shortest path in grid 74, 75

C

checkers
rival, implementing 195–206
collider-based system
used, for hearing function 156-160
used, for seeing function 154, 155
used, for smelling function 160-163
constraints 33
convolution filters
used, for improving influence 141-143

D

decisions
making 91
making, with goal-oriented
behaviors 111-113
decision tree
and finite-state machines (FSM) 100, 101
selecting through 92-94
using 215-219
decomposers 33
Depth-First Search (DFS) algorithm
used, for finding way out of maze 72, 73
Dijkstra algorithm
used, for finding shortest path 75-78
Dirichlet domains
used, for representing world 59

E

editors
URL 68